The Christian Vision:
MAN AND MORALITY

Edited by Thomas J. Burke

The Hillsdale College Press
Hillsdale, Michigan 49242

Hillsdale College Press

Books by George Roche; the *Champions of Freedom* series from the Ludwig von Mises Lecture Series on economic policy; *The Essential Imprimis* collection; the CCA-Shavano video and cassette tapes; and the easy-to-read, humorous *Alternatives* program materials to explain the economic facts of life, are all available from the HILLSDALE COLLEGE PRESS.

General Editor: Lynne Morris

THE CHRISTIAN VISION: MAN AND MORALITY
© 1986 by Hillsdale College Press
Hillsdale, Michigan 49242

Printed in the United States of America

First Printing 1986
Library of Congress Catalog Card Number 85-081263
ISBN 0-916308-96-0

Contents

Foreword

This second volume of our *Christian Vision* book series continues the vision we at Hillsdale finally realized several years ago: the establishment of a permanent program within our academic curriculum devoted to Christian Studies.

The idea for such a program originated in the late 1970s when the estimable scholar Russell Kirk graced our campus as a visiting professor of history and English. Dr. Kirk's proposal for the formation of the program was issued May 20, 1978, and included the signatures of Thomas Howard and Gerhart Niemeyer as well as Sheldon Smith and James Hitchcock.

Six years of planning went into the Christian Studies Program before it became a reality. The multidisciplinary curriculum, offering courses in religion, philosophy, psychology, history, political science, English, and theatre, took another step forward last year when it was approved as an academic major.

Along with its establishment in its second year as a fully developed major, the program was enriched in 1985 by the addition of a talented scholar–teacher, Dr. John Reist, who serves as Professor of Christian Studies and Literature. Dr. Reist has been a welcome addition to the core of able faculty already teaching Christian Studies courses — Dr. Thomas Burke in religion, Drs. John Willson and Warren Treadgold in history, Drs. Thomas Payne and Ralph Hancock in political science, Drs. James Juroe and Benjamin Alexander in English, and Dr. Raymond Pentzell in theatre.

The essays contained in this volume were presented at the first Center for Constructive Alternatives (CCA) seminar of the

1984–85 academic year at Hillsdale College. This week-long seminar series, which takes place four times a year at Hillsdale and is now in its fourteenth year, is recognized nationwide for the consistent quality of its format and speakers.

Now that the first CCA seminar of each academic year is reserved for the exploration of the Judeo-Christian tradition as it relates to some aspect of our society, we are much enthused about the many possibilities for future topics. This fall's seminar dealt with the development of a Christian psychology, and plans are underway for a 1986 seminar that will examine the relationship of faith to the enterprise of athletics.

The Christian Studies Program has further been enriched by the Staley Lecture Series, sponsored by the evangelical Thomas Staley Foundation, under the aegis of the religion and philosophy department. Each year this series invites a distinguished scholar to the Hillsdale campus to present papers dealing with topics in religion and philosophy.

The goal of the Christian Studies Program is to enable interested students to recognize and appreciate the influence of Christianity upon Western culture and to understand their rights and responsibilities within the culture; to equip students for constructive evaluation of their own moral and spiritual values; and to inform students about Christian teachings concerning God and man's relationship to Him.

The program is also non-denominational. The faculty represent most of the major Christian faiths, and guest lecturers include representatives of non-Christian traditions as well. This same spirit of free inquiry was set forth by the 1844 Baptist founders when they chartered the school.

It is my hope that you find inspiration and spiritual food for thought in the essays contained herein. May they also challenge you to ponder the influence the greatest Book ever written has had upon us not only as a society but as individuals as well.

George Roche
Hillsdale, Michigan

Introduction

A unique characteristic of human societies and civilizations consists in their moral dimension. Even though there exist among all cultures many similarities and agreements on various moral questions and principles, each civilization has had its own distinctive moral outlook founded upon its own particular metaphysical perspective. This is not to say that the moral framework of a society is evenly distributed or that its imperatives and their implications are so sharply focused that ambiguities and equivocal situations do not frequently arise. Indeed, a great deal of legal and legislative energy goes into sharpening moral principles and determining their proper application.

It is a historical truism that Western civilization's moral and evaluative roots lie in a blend of Greco-Roman and Hebraic-Christian cultures. Augustine molded and explicated Christian faith with the aid of Platonic philosophical tools, forming the foundation for the intellectual development of the Middle Ages. Aquinas and the scholastic tradition in general took this Augustinian tradition and created a grand synthesis with the newly introduced philosophical system of Aristotle. The disintegration of the scholastic systems of the late Middle Ages and the resurgent biblicism of the Reformation were soon accompanied by attempts to formulate ethical world views which were not directly derived from the Bible of the Church's philosophical and theological tradition. It can be safely said, however, that until the late nineteenth century, most of these non-theological approaches presumed the same general moral outlook as the theologians. There was a common core of moral and ethical principles that was taken for granted, and most disagreement concerned either their proper foundation and origin or their relative importance and priority. These differences were not unimportant, for not every moral viewpoint gave the same emphasis or importance to the same principles. Nevertheless, sufficient agreement existed over fundamental values to give Western society the unity and coherence necessary to make it an identifiable tradition.

In the last 100 years, however, these foundational values themselves, previously considered invaluable and irrevocable, have been seriously and radically challenged by Marxist and secular interpretations of history, Darwinian and naturalistic theories of the natural order, and Freudian and behavioristic beliefs about the nature of man.

Individual freedom, the ultimate worth of the individual in particular and of humankind in general, the dignity of work, and sexual mores are just some of the values whose traditional understanding and/or validity have been questioned and often rejected for alternatives. The following articles, first delivered at our fall, 1984 Center for Constructive Alternatives seminar, "The Bible and Traditional Western Values," examine the relationship between our Western axiological tradition and its religious roots. To what extent is our understanding of values derived from and dependent upon the Bible? What, indeed, are the fundamental values developed in the Bible and how do they differ from those current in ancient Greece or modern America? Are these values relevant, important, and valid in today's world, or do we need to search for new foundations and new values? Can the "Christian world view" adequately answer the attacks mounted against it in the twentieth century? These and other important questions are addressed herein.

These essays can provide, of course, only an introductory and general treatment. The issues are so broad and the historical and philosophical interrelationships so complex and intricate that any pretense of finality would be outrageous. But given the intended audience and the limits imposed by format and space, we have sought to establish at least a preliminary case for a positive evaluation of our traditional moral heritage and its vital dependence on biblical beliefs and faith. We have included two articles which specifically focus on the Bible, "The God of the Bible and Moral Foundations," by Carl F. H. Henry and my own, "The Fundamental Principles of Biblical Ethics."

In the first essay, Henry argues that only by grounding morality in the eternal, revealing, and personal God proclaimed by the Judeo-Christian tradition will there be provided the sort of objectivity and moral imperative necessary to sustain a private and public morality which both maintains individual dignity and worth and, at the same time, also supports community among men at the social and political level. Only the infinite and holy God who has revealed Himself and His will in the Bible supplies an adequate ground for ethical knowledge and moral behavior. Wedding morality to the God of the Bible, Henry avers, solves both the ontological and the epistemological problems facing all moral theories. In Henry's view, morality is objective and unchanging (non-relative), for the God from whom it derives is eternally and unchangingly present; moral truth is also knowable because this God has clearly and intelligibly revealed His will for man propositionally in scripture and personally in Jesus of Nazareth.

It should be noted that the usual handy refutation of "Divine Command Theory" does not work well against Henry's construal of the position. God's will (and thus His commands) is moral because God himself is moral. It is not an abstract and arbitrary will which commands, but the will of a perfectly holy and infinitely benevolent Being. God's will is good because God is good. The question of why one should obey God's will then becomes the question of why one should do the good. But that is a question which no moral theory *qua* moral theory can answer, unless "ought" can be derived from "is" — in which case Henry's "is" can no less validly be the foundation for his "oughts" than those of any other theory.

Henry's purpose is to show that our Western moral sensibilities are as a matter of historical fact derived from the Judeo-Christian view of God and that the removal of that God from the consciousness of Western man means the removal of the implicit foundation for his ethical beliefs. Thus, he elaborates the various alternatives to a theistically based ethics which have been propounded in the past century and points out that they are either relativistic, in which case there can be no common ethical framework for society as a whole which can obligate all its members, or they must rely on intuition of some sort—a precarious venture at best. In the end, of course, non-theistically grounded ethics tend toward either individualistic positions such as egoism or one of the numerous totalitarian-isms. The former deny man's communality and mutual responsibility, while the latter despoil him of his individual dignity and value as a person created in the image of God. In short, Henry's argument is that only a moral system grounded in the eternal and articulate God of the Bible will adequately deal with the full range of human nature and life. Systems grounded in a truncated view of God or in no god at all will inevitably truncate an essential aspect of man's being and, consequently, his life. This inevitability derives from the fact that man has been created in God's image; his full humanity, then, will only be given full justice if ordered in accord with the fullness of the being and revelation of the God in whose image he has been made.

In the second half of his paper, Henry goes on to elaborate on the specifically New Testament view of the moral life. He shows how the New Testament grounds true morality in the knowledge of God and the sanctifying work of the Holy Spirit within the individual believer. The New Testament, he explains, founds the moral life upon the work of the crucified and risen Christ, places it within the context of the knowledge of God, roots it in the regenerating power of the Spirit of God, and defines it in terms of God's *agape*. Christian ethics is, then, Henry holds, dependent on God's salvific plan by which he is restoring within man the *imago Dei*. Only a return to the transcendent ethics of the Bible, he concludes, will keep modern man from foundering upon either its humanistic perversions or its naturalistic substitutes.

In my article, I attempt to outline the fundamental factors

for which any Christian theory of ethics will have to account if it is to claim biblical support. Naturally, this is not an attempt to outline a fully developed theory of Christian ethics. But it is claimed that there are at least seven pairs of polar concepts, the exclusion of any of which will ultimately fault one's ethical theory. In fact, it seems to me that the basic shortcomings in all past moral theories lie in their exclusion or diminution of one or more of these polarities or in the undue accenting of one member of a pair over the other. In so doing, an essential and vital aspect of human existence is given an inadequate role in ethical decision-making or valuation; but any finally satisfactory ethical theory cannot leave out or unduly diminish a virtue which is grounded in some uneliminable part of our nature and life. The seven polarities herein described are an attempt, then, to outline the basic principles one finds used or taught in the Bible as factors which, when relevant to the ethical situation under consideration, are to be considered criteria of divinely approved, proscribed or prescribed behavior.

Ethical viewpoints which look to the Bible as their fundamental source for values, rules and principles have been severely challenged since the Enlightenment. Attempts to form alternative ethical views have arisen within both modern existentialism and twentieth-century analytic philosophy. Two of our papers, therefore, seek to address these perspectives. These are not, it should be noted, merely negative or polemical evaluations. While forcefully arguing for the ultimate validity of the Judeo-Christian tradition, they also recognize that contributions to that tradition are to be found in philosophers who on the whole reject it. Moreover, any native reaction to any culture is going to draw from that culture itself, challenging the dominance of certain assumptions and values by means of others. Consequently, the defense of tradition does not necessarily entail a wholesale rejection of everything its opponents hold. In "The Existentialist Challenge to Christian Values: Sheer Freedom or Shaped Faith?", John Reist points out that existentialism has a Christian as well as an atheistic expression, and that, indeed, some of the most penetrating insights of existentialism come from men such as Pascal and Kierkegaard.

Reist analyzes existentialism under the four rubrics of participation, personalism, presentism, and possibility. He lays open the two major shortcomings in atheistic existentialism: its flight from reason and its attempt to define life in terms of will alone. By denying objective truth, rejecting revealed truth, and expelling completely any thought of man as created in the *imago Dei*, atheistic existentialism undermines the value and dignity of man which must be presupposed in any viable and compelling ethics. Reist calls first for an affirmation of personal value based on an objective meaning for human life established by God in creation, and second for commitment to neighbor, community, and tradition on the basis of objective truth about human life revealed by God through scripture. In short, the answer to the emptiness generated by "sheer freedom" is faith shaped neither by the ultimately fatalistic pretensions of rationalism nor the pure subjectivity of existentialist voluntarism, but by the God revealed derivatively through scripture and tradition and pre-eminently through Jesus Christ. The will of man can only be "true" when guided by the truth about man.

In "Analytic Ethics in the Twentieth Century," Keith Yandell presents a brief synopsis of the developments in analytic ethics from intuitionism, emotivism, and prescriptivism to a renewal of interest in traditional ethical views. The relentless self-criticism which analytic philosophy practices has enabled at least some of its exponents to see the deep problems in modern ethical theories and to consider traditional moral viewpoints as viable alternatives.

After a brief historical summary from Moore to Hare, Yandell brings out the strengths and weaknesses of utilitarianism, probably the most pervasive ethical view of twentieth-century analytic philosophers. He argues that it cannot, finally, provide us with an adequate basis for ethics or a satisfactory ethical theory. Its weaknesses, according to Yandell, are both theoretical and practical. In effect, he argues, a "Simon pure" utilitarianism surreptitiously introduces other moral principles, thereby undermining the claim that utility is the fundamental principle of ethical action.

Yandell points out that the revival of rational ethics has involved the placing of ethical theory within the broader context of metaphysics (the nature of the world in general and human action in particular) and the willingness to interact with traditional ethics, including the Judeo-Christian tradition. Thus, it appears that at least some of those nurtured on the analytic tradition have begun to see the need for a theory of human nature and the nature of the world for a viable theory of ethics. The Judeo-Christian tradition, of course, provides such a foundation and, therefore, is a source to which some are turning. Perhaps the greatest contribution of the Judeo-Christian tradition, Yandell proffers, is its emphasis upon persons as bearers of ultimate ethical value, an insight which even that tradition has not always maintained as central. Yandell concludes that the most promising future for modern ethical theory lies in the development of that ethical tradition which has its roots in the biblical scriptures and the history of Christian reflection upon them.

The most serious challenge to Christianity today comes from Marxism, in many ways a sort of heretical breakoff from our ecclesiastical tradition. The central thrust of Marxism focuses on economics, and so in "Political-Economic Freedom and the Biblical Ethic," Ronald Nash analyzes the ethical implications of all forms of centralized and/or government-controlled economic systems and contrasts them with biblical teachings on the dignity and freedom of man. In particular, he is concerned to respond to those within the church who somehow find capitalism unjust and argue that Christians are morally obligated to opt for socialistic or communistic solutions to the economic problems confronting modern developed and undeveloped societies.

Nash first outlines those aspects of the biblical world view which he considers relevant to the issues, namely, man's stewardship status regarding worldly possessions, his God-given rights and freedoms, basic biblical ethical principles, and "the inescapable fact of human sin and depravity." He then argues that it is capitalism, not Marxism or any of its socialistic alternatives, that is most compatible with the Christian world view as a whole. The incompatibility of Christianity with Marxist and socialist economic systems, Nash argues, derives primarily from the violent and compulsory natures of the latter and the dissolution of human rights and liberties which inevitably follow their establishment.

After this negative evaluation of socialism, Nash goes on to argue for the essential compatibility of capitalism with Christianity. Capitalism, and limited government in general, Nash insists, provide the sort of economic and political environment in which a biblically based notion of human nature can flourish, while at the same time they provide the best possible constraints on human depravity and wickedness. In other words, they allow the development of essential biblical virtues without losing sight of the biblical teaching on sin and alienation.

Nash closes with a brief analysis of what he considers the flawed exegetical methods of contemporary liberation theologians. Their hermeneutical procedures result in the disastrous combination of bad theology with bad economics. He concludes that for one who seeks to strive for the ennoblement of man in accord with the biblical vision, the choice between capitalism and all forms of socialism and Marxism leaves him no rational, theological, or moral option but the former.

Liberation theologians draw heavily upon the Bible and the early Church Fathers to support their position. In "Market and Money in Jewish and Christian Thought in the Hellenistic and Roman Ages," Leonard Liggio examines the teaching of the Old and New Testaments and the early Church Fathers on the subject of wealth. He argues that the facile condemnation of "the rich," capitalism, and Western society in general by liberation theologians is merely based upon a Marxist analysis of man and society, and that the support of the Bible and the Church Fathers is achieved only by an uncritical and superficial reading of the texts. In a paper of this length and format, his own examination is not itself, of course, a prolonged, scholarly, exegetical study, but a presentation of his conclusions on the import of biblical and early church teaching in this area. Certainly, however, the issues he raises, the contextual information he provides, and the alternative construals he proposes should make it clear that the interpretations of liberation theology are highly suspect and in need of critical re-examination.

Liggio's paper should stimulate intense study of ancient Hebrew, Roman, and Greek culture. He paves the way for a more positive and affirming acceptance of wealth *per se* and a more satisfying understanding of the biblical and patristic texts in regard to this topic than the condemnatory, pietistic, and ascetical pronouncements to which liberation theology adheres. Indeed, Liggio argues that it is the very emphasis on taxation and centralized, autocratic and pervasive government control which forms the background to many of the patristic condemnations of the rich and their abuse of power and wealth. Consequently, he argues, a return to a centralized and controlled socialistic economy can hardly be the means to bringing society in line with gospel. Liggio also points to the utopianism implicit in liberation theology and the fundamental contradiction between its this-worldly, societal vision of salvation and the church's traditional emphasis on the spiritual and individual as the locus and focal point of the Kingdom of God.

Another pressing question in today's pluralistic society concerns the degree to which any religiously based ethical viewpoint ought to be allowed to influence society as a whole. In "Catholic Social Thought, Virtue and Public Morality," J. Brian Benestad presents a statement of traditional Roman Catholic teaching regarding the relations of religion and morality to public policy and legislation. In the first major section of his paper, he treats the question of ecclesiastical pronouncements on matters of public morality and policy. The Church, through the office of the bishops, he argues, has traditionally spoken out on such subjects, particularly on questions regarding the common good. Given the Thomistic division of nature and grace, there is no reason why Catholic teaching regarding the best modes of human conduct in the former, based upon reason alone, should not be part of the public debate on relevant issues. Moreover, he argues, in its evangelizing office, the Church also has a duty to speak out on such matters. Thus, statements on matters of public policy such as the recent bishops' letters on war and peace and on the economy are not improper *per se*. Benestad does, however, find fault with the emphasis on explicit policy and the lack of attention to fundamental moral principles and values. Moreover, he notes the mistaken assumption in these letters that somehow legislation can bring out a just, equitable and virtuous society. Cultural consensus, he points out, cannot be revised like the tax code — an assumption explicitly stated in the bishops' letter on the economy.

In the second major section, Benestad addresses the problem of relating a Christian view of virtue to the common good. To what extent can and to what extent cannot the Christian address the moral and ethical issues confronting society? Recognizing that not every matter of personal morality is a proper subject for legislation, he argues that nevertheless even religiously based morality has a proper place in the public forum. When issues have a direct effect on the common good, the Christian must address them. He uses the vexing question of abortion to show how the lines ought and ought not to be drawn between those matters in which belief and practice ought to remain private and those which ought to be addressed and decided publicly, regardless of the origin of the moral convictions by which the decision is reached. He concludes by briefly outlining four arguments against the continued allowance of abortion on demand. Throughout this presentation, he emphasizes the common good — as opposed to individual rights — as the proper primary determinant in the formation of a public morality and its responsible and legitimate imposition through legislation.

We conclude with James Hitchcock's paper, "Catholics and Evangelicals: A New Era?", which highlights the new realignment in theological affinities created by the rise of liberal Christianity and leftist political and economic viewpoints within both Roman Catholicism and Protestantism. At one point in history, no two religious communities were more opposed to one another than Evangelical Protestants and Roman Catholics, the former stressing *sola scriptura, sola fides*, and personal conversion; the latter emphasizing the hierarchical, sacramental, and authoritarian nature of the Church and its consequent indispensability for salvation. Hitchcock, it should be noted, does not say these differences are unimportant or resolved. But recognizing the reality and legitimacy of both theological traditions he argues that the rise of a third, alternative tradition within both has shown that underlying the strong disagreements is a body of common beliefs which are even more fundamental. Indeed, he sees this new tradition, which has at its core the thesis of the relativity and consequent questioning of any and all authority, on the one hand, and the rejection of the transcendent, revelatory activity of God, on the other hand, as in fundamental opposition to any form of Christianity properly so called. As G. Gresham Machen argued fifty years previously, it is actually another religion.

Roman Catholicism and Evangelicalism owe to liberalism a perception of their own agreement. Consequently, Hitchcock holds out the hope of a truly constructive ecumenism between them, an ecumenism founded on commonly held theological convictions which, nevertheless, does not compromise where real disagreements exist. He recognizes that such cooperation will more likely be in the area of action, promoting policies and moral standards which both traditions honor, while each retains its traditional theological stance. But such ecumenism, he concludes, will be more vital and lasting than one which relativizes dogma, considering it a mere human attempt to plumb the divine and in need of constant revision in light of whatever "ism" arises next on the horizon. Indeed, Hillsdale College's Christian Studies Program was originated and has been developed by this same alliance, and the strength and depth of that program is witness to the validity of Hitchcock's position. He gives clear and cogent expression to the "ecumenism" for which Hillsdale stands and in accord with which it operates.

It is hoped these essays will provoke thought, discussion, and a renewed appreciation of our classical Judeo-Christian tradition and its perspective, particularly as that tradition speaks to fundamental issues of morality and human life. The West is in urgent need of finding a reason for its continuance. Disillusionment is so rampant in most of Europe that population decline is dramatic; the West is becoming a civilization without purpose and, consequently, without the vital energy necessary to will its own future existence. The young are adopting selfish and egoistic idols, myths of fulfillment through "self-actualization," financial success, even drugs and, occasionally, fanatical causes which condone and promote terrorist acts against society itself. These are substituted for the transcendent values which have enriched and ennobled our culture for millennia, and their rise has been accompanied with the usual symptoms manifested by disintegrating civilizations. We hope these essays will spark not only interest in, but also allegiance to those values and that grand tradition which, if they capture the minds and imaginations of forthcoming generations, can reawaken and strengthen true virtue and justice in our modern era, and rekindle our civilization's development towards a culture which rightly honors man's divinely bestowed dignity and thereby the Creator Himself.

Thomas J. Burke
Hillsdale College

The God of the Bible and Moral Foundations

Carl F. H. Henry

Dr. Carl F. H. Henry, Lecturer-at-Large for World Vision International, was Distinguished Visiting Professor of Christian Studies, Hillsdale College, during the fall of 1983 and the spring and fall of 1984. He received his undergraduate degree from Wheaton College and earned doctorates from Boston University and the Northern Baptist Theological Seminary. Dr. Henry has been professor of theology at both Northern and Eastern Baptist Seminaries and at Fuller Seminary. He has held numerous visiting professorships at colleges and universities throughout the world. Past president of the American Theological Society, he was founding editor of the influential evangelical fortnightly, *Christianity Today*, which he edited for 12 years. He is the author of hundreds of articles, 28 books, and editor of 11 more. Having completed his massive six-volume analysis of contemporary theological systems and thought, *God, Revelation and Authority*, he also recently published *The Christian Mindset in a Secular Age*. He is now in the process of writing his autobiography.

It is impossible to contemplate traditional Western values without reference to the God of the Bible. The ideals that lifted the West above ancient paganism had their deepest source and support in the self-revealed God who was and is for Christians the *summum bonum* or supreme good.

Nowhere is the singular uniqueness of the God of the Bible more evident than in the Christian vision of the good and the right that Scripture commends and nurtures. One need only recall the biblical basis of many long-accepted beliefs about the moral order. Among these are the convictions that God is intrinsically moral and the sovereign source of all ethical dis-

1

tinctions; that a comprehensive moral purpose pervades all human history; that the articulately revealed will of the Creator embraces all matters private and public (including human relationships to fellow-humans, to the state and to the cosmos); that *agape* is both the nature of God and the prime human virtue; that life even in the womb is God's gift and that human existence gains its fixed worth from creation in the *imago Dei*; that Jesus of Nazareth incarnates the very life, truth and holy love of God; that the kingdom of God and its blessings are mercifully accessible to sinful humanity through the crucified and risen Jesus who controls the sluicegates of eternity; and that through its unyielding call to the justice and justification of God, the regenerate church as the New Society is to reflect worldwide the joys and privileges of the kingdom of God through its witness to redemptive good news and new life.

I

The God of the Bible is the self-revealing infinite Spirit. He is the sovereign source of all other being. He is the authoritative and purposive ruler of nature and history, the specifier of a worthy way of life and ordainer of the community of faith. He stands at the commencement of a flawlessly created cosmos, one which at every stage of its origination He as its Maker declares to be good. When a subsequently rebellious race seeks in Adam autonomously to redefine truth and the good, He mercifully offers salvation; in the incarnate Logos or Second Adam He provides redemption for the penitent. He is the God of holy love. At the end of world history He will stand victorious amid the Omega-fortunes of the nations and of mankind, and in final judgment He will decisively doom evil and eternally vindicate righteousness.

II

Now and again in the long history of speculative thought, philosophers have vigorously disputed one or another perfection that the Bible predicates of the living God. During the last century, for example, novel metaphysical theories called into question virtually every facet of the Christian definition of God. Philosophers debated whether God is personal, whether He is infinite, whether He is distinct from the cosmos, whether He is unchanging, whether He is all-powerful and all-knowing and all-wise, whether He transcends time, whether He is loving, and even in what sense He may be regarded as the God of truth.

But in the recent past, humanists (as many naturalists now prefer to call themselves) have boldly repudiated God's very existence as a transcendent personal Being. When John Dewey deplored supernaturalism a generation ago as a noxious faith and proposed replacing Judeo-Christian religion by a naturalistic humanism,[1] he nonetheless confusingly retained the term God (for the interaction between the ideal and actual). The more recent contemporary humanist Paul Kurtz, however, urges us to "weed out permanently the idea of God."[2]

Naturalism reduces all reality to impersonal processes and events. It assails not simply this or that particular article of Christian belief, but rejects the very possibility of a credible theistic faith. Naturalism mythologizes the basic theses of biblical theism, namely, God, creation, revelation, redemption and judgment.

Because nontheistic world views have now pervasively penetrated contemporary culture — most notably public education, the mass media, and political decision — belief in the God of the Bible no longer governs the Western intellectual's conceptions of truth and goodness, nor does it shape contemporary society's view of liberty and love, or of responsibility and right. Although contemporary humanists champion an agenda of

---

[1]John Dewey, *A Common Faith* (New Haven: Yale University Press, 1934).
[2]Paul Kurtz, *The Fullness of Life* (New York: Horizon Press, 1974), p. 16.

social ethics, their proposals involve little more than a pirating of selected aspects of biblical morality that are totally unrelated to a naturalistic theory of the universe.

Earlier in this century the historian F. A. Foakes-Jackson remarked that all the West's distinctive virtues stem from the evangelical theology of the Cross. The current revolt against a supernaturally grounded morality therefore poses something of an enigma for contemporary ethical theory. Philosophical skepticism and moral relativism have engulfed ever-wider reaches of modern life until a sweeping civilizational crisis now overshadows the West. Not only do theorists who try to sustain moral imperatives independently of God disagree over the ultimate sanction of morals, but they also fail to provide any truly objective basis for their conclusions about the good and the right. Naturalism's inability to sustain fixed ethical principles is nowhere more apparent than in its many contradictory attempts since the Renaissance to fashion a humanistic ethics, and in its increasing tendency to justify and even to praise immorality.

III

In the biblical outlook God as the Creator of all existence and Lord of life gives a unifying focus to human thought and action. Only in the context of the living God and of His moral purpose in the universe do we find the reason for man's being. "If God, the creator, *is*," Emil Brunner remarks, "then the gloomy idea of fate and fatality which lies like a spell over the ancient as well as the modern world, loses its basis. It is not a fate, an impersonal abstract determining power, . . . which is above everything that is and happens, but He, the creator spirit, the creator person."[3] In consequence, as Arthur F. Holmes

---

[3] Emil Brunner, *Christianity and Civilization* (London: Nisbet, 1948), p. 18.

observes, biblical monotheism "involves a theology and an ethic that affected every kind of human activity."[4]

IV

To be sure, even the polytheistic gods were viewed by the ancients as trafficking in ethical concerns. But, as Nahum Sarna observes, these gods were "innately capricious"; "their ethical quality was but one of many diverse and contradictory attributes and was neither inherent in the idea of the godhead nor absolute." By contrast, says Sarna, morality and ethics "constitute the very essence" of the God of the Bible; his transcendent "thou shalt not" permeates all human history brought into being by the Creator's sovereign will.[5]

In the Bible God is Himself the Good and He declares His original creation to be essentially good. God's commandments articulate and summarize His will for His creatures, and by this His own righteous standard He judges all people and nations. He suspends our destiny in eternity on our response to His law and to Jesus Christ "the just and holy one."

For Plato, the Good was independent of God and was normative for the Demiurge who according to Plato gave form to the universe.[6] But for the Bible nothing is absolutely independent of God; everything is dependent on Him. Augustine, Duns Scotus and the Protestant Reformers insisted that God Himself decrees the good. Luther affirmed that what God wills "is not right because He ought or was bound, so to will; on the contrary, what takes place must be right because He so wills it."[7] Some of the early modern philosophers — notably Descartes,

---

[4]Arthur F. Holmes, *Contours of a World View* (Grand Rapids: Wm. B. Eeerdmans Publishing Co., 1983), p. 7.

[5]Nahum Sarna, "Understanding Creation in Genesis," in *Is God a Creationist?*, ed. by Roland Mushat Frye (New York: Charles Scribner's Sons, 1983), pp. 168 ff.

[6]Plato *Euthyphro* 9e.

[7]Martin Luther, *The Bondage of the Will*, Ch. 5, Sec. IV.

Locke and Berkeley—also affirmed divine-command morality. As for the neo-orthodox theologians Karl Barth and Emil Brunner, they, too, formally retained a divine-command ethics but muted its propositional content by correlating the divine confrontational demand with private faith and decision.

Modern philosophy, for which the nature and then the very existence of God became problematical, increasingly disavowed divine-command ethics. John Stuart Mill and J. M. E. McTaggart rejected biblical theism in part because it affirms that the good is what God wills. Today even many professing theists no longer consider the statement that "God wills" something to be an ethical pronouncement. Divine-command morality is even identified with a "might is right" mentality. The current view— shared by many mediating theologians—is, as Jeffrey Stout observes, that morality is autonomous; it is "logically independent from both theoretical reason and theology."[8]

This revolt against the Christian heritage has meant the loss both of an ethically significant view of God and of a stable morality. Recent modern attempts to ground ethics in intuition or in utility or some other sociological factor merely collapse morality into psychology. If applied consistently to ethics, naturalism erodes any external foundation of morality and reduces values to subjectivity. Ethical claims become merely culture-relative, for an evolving humanity decides what truth and morality signify at any moment.

So confused is the contemporary pursuit of moral imperatives that academics are probing and discussing divine-command morality anew for light on the loss of an objective ethic. G. E. M. Anscombe, for example, declares that morality is indispensably rooted in the presuppositions of biblical theism; indeed, she insists, obligation statements make sense only in a divine law conception of ethics.[9] Janine Marie Idziak has

---

[8]Jeffrey Stout, *The Flight from Authority* (Notre Dame: University of Notre Dame Press, 1981), p. ix.

[9]G. E. M. Anscombe, "Modern Moral Philosophy," *Philosophy*, 33 (January, 1958), p. 8.

recently gathered essays, some previously untranslated, that promote and defend the traditional view.[10] Erstwhile champions of natural law theory are being confronted by their contemporaries with the biblical emphasis that the law of god is an articulate revelatory provision.

What distinguished ancient Israel from her pagan neighbor-nations in the Near East was her knowledge of the revealed will of Yahweh and her commitment to live responsibly in view of his divine commandments. In contrast with Hittite, Egyptian, Babylonian, Canaanite and Philistine cultures, there arose in consequence, as Eric Voegelin remarks, "a new society, set off from the civilizations of the age" and "living toward a goal beyond history. . . . Here was a people that began its existence in history with a radical leap in being," one that reversed the postulations of social evolution, according to which "a society is supposed to start from primitive myths and advance gradually," whereas Israel began "where a respectable society has difficulties even ending."[11] The supposedly superior modern view, that God is answerable to moral norms approved by an evolved and enlightened humanity, has led by contrast to the ethical collapse of contemporary civilization and to moral futility.

V

Among the great world religions, only Judaism, Christianity and Islam depict the deity as the sovereign God who speaks intelligibly, a doctrine that Islam, moreover, clearly inherited from the Judeo-Christian Scriptures. Secular philosophy, even where it champions speculative theism, is hostile to this emphasis on transcendent rational revelation in order to advance phil-

---

[10]Janine Marie Idziak, *Divine Command Morality: Historical and Contemporary Readings* (New York: The Edwin Mellon Press, 1979).

[11]Eric Voegelin, *Israel and Revelation* (Baton Rouge: Louisiana State University Press, 1956), pp. 113, 315 ff.

osophical reasoning as an alternative way of knowing metaphysical and moral reality. But speculative philosophy has bred logically contradictory views and now even obscures the very meaning of meaning. The recent past has spawned irrationalistic philosophies and religions, most notably existentialism and mysticism. It tells much about such modern alternatives that their most vigorous complaint against the biblical heritage is that orthodox theism appeals for cognitive consent and logical consistency.

The God of the Bible communicates His thought and word intelligibly. He addresses the human mind and conscience through external nature and history, universally confronting humanity's sullied but still surviving *imago Dei* with the knowledge of his transcendent divinity (Rom. 1:18 ff.) and reminding sinful mankind that the human revolt against light invites inescapable judgment (Rom. 1:32). God makes known His character and will not only in general or universal revelation, but specifically also in His salvific disclosure to his covenant people; this He does, moreover, both in redemptive historical acts and in the inspired and inscripturated prophetic-apostolic interpretation of those acts, and supremely so in the divine incarnation in Jesus Christ.

This fact, of God's articulate disclosure of His moral will in the Decalogue and other ethical imperatives that Scripture publishes in a literary canon, and that Jesus Christ publishes in His life and ministry, has far-reaching consequences. It disputes mystics who would deny intelligibility to divine revelation because of its supernatural character. And it disputes modern rationalists as well, who in the name of evolutionary intelligence consider final divine revelation offensive to the modern mind. No one should be surprised that such commentators, shrouding God as they do in metaphysical obscurity, often propound mythopoetical views of revelation, and that this defamation of divine disclosure involves in turn a loss of the ontological foundations of Christian faith.

The Bible teaches that the one living and self-disclosed God is all-wise and self-consistent. This doctrine of the unity, wisdom and self-consistency of God "was impressed upon Western civilization," says John Jefferson Davis, "only after a long and arduous struggle with Greek, Roman and barbarian polytheism."[12] Now in our own time novel theories of divinity are once again disputing divine wisdom and self-consistency, tenets of great importance to basic aspects of Judeo-Christian doctrine such as revelation, creation, providence, redemption and eschatology. Process theology views God as a divinity growing in knowledge; its insistence that God is an aspect of all reality leads, moreover, to the notion that divinity striates even the realm of evil. Dialectical theology views God as a deity who eludes rational synthesis; emphasizing an inner divine command, it deprives the biblical commandments of their proper status as rational propositional revelation. It is impossible, from such views, to derive a comprehensive, intelligibly consistent outlook either on God's essential moral nature or on the ideal content of the moral life.

VI

The biblical view insistently declares God to be the sole sovereign of the universe: creator, preserver, governor and judge. The Decalogue (Exodus 20) relates all the ethical demands impinging upon man and society to the will and purpose of the one living God. The implications of God's universal sovereignty extend to every sphere of life and thought.

The dominion over nature that God has assigned to man (Gen. 1:26; Ps. 8:6) entails human sensitivity to the Creator's moral and spiritual purposes for our planet. It is this biblical emphasis on human dominion that secular theories have unjustifiably blamed at times for the plunder and exploitation of natural resources. Christians may indeed not always have fully implemented ecological responsibilities but they have at least

---

[12]John Jefferson Davis, *Foundations of Evangelical Theology* (Grand Rapids: Baker Book House, 1984), p. 253.

identified the moral framework that objectively motivates conscience and action. Naturalistic morality on the other hand can neither summon nor vindicate fixed ethical principles of any kind. If *homo sapiens* is essentially but an animal he can hardly be expected to subordinate self-interest to the good of the community. For that reason, even as Christians have brought to the *ad hoc* concern of secular nature-lovers a depth and permanence of protest against cosmic pollution that mere humanism cannot sustain, so now they must also speak up against the littering of outer space by satellite and missile debris.

The implications of divine sovereignty, we said, are far-reaching. Take, for example, the political realm. Aristotle held that human beings — at least in the sphere of politics — belong to the state, a misunderstanding that no scripturally grounded Jew or Christian would hesitate to challenge. According to the Bible the state exists within God's providential will and has limited authority. When totalitarian states presume to define human rights and duties at will they illicitly claim divine prerogatives. The state's biblically stated role is to maintain God-ordained justice, not to devise or manipulate it; as the American charter political documents declare, human beings are "endowed by their Creator with certain inalienable rights." Sad to say, the United Nations Declaration of Human Rights obscures this emphasis on the transcendent supernatural foundation and stipulation of human rights; it does so, moreover, precisely at a time in history when monstrous totalitarian claims are being made by predatory powers.

Religious freedom — that is, one's right to worship and to obey God in good conscience — shelters and nurtures all other human rights, and in this sense undergirds them. Only if human beings have political and civil liberty to worship according to conscience can they worship and serve the living God meaningfully and resist the efforts of arbitrary powers who require subjects to do what God prohibits or to abstain from what God requires. In the absence of individual liberty to worship conscientiously, citizens fall prey to pretentious powers that arrogate to themselves the absolute authority and unqualified honor reserved only to God. The example of the Christian apostles, who when thwarted by civil authorities in fulfilling the Great Commission preferred physical imprisonment to spiritual disobedience ("We must obey God rather than man," Acts 5:29, N.E.B.), remains normative for Christians even today.

Humanists hostile to revealed religion frequently cite instances of gross intolerance and persecution within the course of religious history such as the ancient Hebrew extinction of pagan neighbors in the name of Yahweh, the medieval Crusades, the Inquisition, and even the religious wars of recent modern times, including Islam's reliance on the sword to extend Koranic influence. This lamentable record is not offset by simply noting that the Bible nowhere exonerates persecutors that darken the annals of Christendom, be they nonbelievers or believers.

We should remind humanist critics, however, that world history records no persecution and inhumanity more debased and cruel than that waged against theists and dissenters under the banner of atheistic philosophies and rulers. Examples include the Hitler regime's murder of 6 million Jews and vast numbers of Gentiles; Stalin's destruction of some 15 million Russians; and Mao's approved murder of some 25 million Chinese. Nothing in the entire history of mankind can match this twentieth-century brutality, in a time frame that scientific naturalism extols for its technocratic genius and as the pinnacle of human progress.

Religious freedom is in fact and in essence a Christian priority. It should say something to all world religions that in the United States, which has no state religion, voluntary religion has nurtured a predominantly theistic citizenry whose vigorous evangelistic and humanitarian outreach to the world is unrivaled among the nations.

VII

God's love in the biblical model has nurtured and unleashed a veritable floodtide of compassion in human history. In Judeo-Christian Scripture divine love is not *eros* or interest in an object for self-serving ends, but rather *agape*, an outgoing affection that confers upon the needy an unmerited benefit. The supreme example of *agape* is the Father's salvific gift of the divine Son and Redeemer: "God so loved the world that He gave His one and only Son, that whosoever believes in Him shall not perish but have everlasting life" (John 3:16, N.I.V.). Every one of the extended references to divine *agape* in the New Testament epistles focuses on the Cross, that is, on the Savior's substitutionary atonement for sinners.

The *agape* of God, as Anders Nygren remarks, "reverses natural human valuation."[13] That Christ died for us while we were yet sinners and in fact enemies of God has injected into human relationships a motivation that neither speculative philosophy nor empirical science nor humanistic education has managed to engender or maintain. Biblical theism has stimulated an unprecedented manifestation of compassionate concern for the weak, the needy and the helpless.

More than fifty years ago Robert A. Millikan said of science that it filled mankind with new vision and hope and striving for a better human existence, one that somewhat broadened human concern "from individual-soul salvation to race salvation."[14] In a still earlier work he had observed that "by definitely introducing the most stimulating and inspiring motive for altruistic effort which has ever been introduced, namely the motive arising from the conviction that we ourselves may be the vital agents in the march of things, science has provided a reason for altruistic effort which is quite independent of the ultimate destination of the individual and is also much more alluring to some

---

[13]Anders Nygren, *Agape and Eros*, Vol. II (London: S.P.C.K., 1963), p. 39.
[14]Robert A. Millikan, *Science and the New Civilization* (New York: Charles Scribner's Sons, 1931), p. 78.

sorts of minds than singing hosannas forever around the throne."[15]

But as modern intellectuals have sought to find in this present world the religious values that earlier generations had found in the divine revelation of another world, moral principles have yielded to utility and expedience. The enormous potential of scientific technology, fusing theory and practice for unprecedented possibilities of control and change, has meanwhile vastly maximized human possibilities not only for good but also for evil. Nothing is more apparent in an age whose prized scientific methodology cannot identify objective values than its need for moral guidelines.

Whereas theistic scholars had patiently investigated the validity of ethical judgments, their present-day naturalistic successors replace such study of the *ought* by interest in the cultural history of moral concerns. Contemporary thought readily accommodates Feuerbach's notion that God is but man's own moral nature posited as absolute being, for a perpetually changing universe necessarily implies a changing humanity with changing ethics. The exaltation of inordinate self-interest at the expense of shared concern for humanity is a popular characteristic as well of modern life; not only Madison Avenue entrepreneurs but contemporary philosophers and clinical counselors also defend and even advocate blatant egoism. The grim specter of a crumbling society poised for self-destruction has vanquished the once alluring vision of a scientific millennium. Self-centered moral philosophy disinterested in the character and purpose of the Creator-Redeemer God severs human beings from the dignity and worth of their true selfhood.

Today's preoccupation with *eros* therefore has costly consequences for family and society. To conjectural philosophers gifted with a special capacity for logical inconsistency the thesis that human beings, even if chance byproducts of naturalistic evolution, should live by theistic principles of morality may

---

[15]Robert A. Millikan, *Evolution in Science and Religion* (New Haven: New York University Press, 1927), pp. 83 f.

seem strangely compelling. But for ordinary mortals the atheistic denial of God and of eternal values and of a future life becomes an open sesame to selfishness and sensuality.

Inherent in the historically given Word and Act of God is a creative moral power that philosophical speculation about human oughtness is powerless to impart. Among His covenant people the self-revealing Creator God nurtured compassion for the weak and helpless, concern for the destitute and needy, and solicitude for the stranger and outcast. A secular society may for a time shift to government the revealed responsibility of individuals, but an empirical perspective that mythologizes the existence of God will inevitably erode the foundations of biblical *agape* and default on its moral implications.

IX

In the United States alone abortion kills more than a million and a half fetuses annually. For contemporary society this issue perhaps more than any other distills the choice between yielding all sexual concerns either to hedonistic indulgence and its consequences or to disciplined evaluation of human life and compassion for the weak and helpless.

Christianity does not measure human life simply by its functional value to society. Human worth is fixed by divine creation in the *imago Dei*, and Christ's redemptive death, moreover, proclaims man's worth even in a sinful condition. Functional worth to society is therefore not the prime question to be raised about the survival of the genetically unwanted or disadvantaged, any more than private sexual pleasure, individual convenience, the cultural mindset or totalitarian decree are to be considered the final determinant in evaluating fetal life.

Human life does not have infinite value, to be sure, for man is both a finite and contingent creature. Divine decree of the death penalty, which declares murder an affront to the divine image (Gen. 9:6), affirms at one and the same time both that human life has immense worth and that this worth can be jeopardized. Whether the fetus is human prior to birth and if so whether its worth begins at conception is a matter of ongoing debate. The contemporary secular view, which champions abortion on demand, differs totally from the Roman Catholic view which now assigns the fetus full personhood from the very moment of conception. In the secular view the fetus is not truly human until the time of birth; its preservation or destruction therefore is essentially only the mother's or at most the parents' decision. The fact is, that most abortions today are rationalized in terms of personal and pragmatic considerations; the mother's and/or mate's preference is the determining factor, and not some transcendent moral principle.

The biblical outlook indicts head-on all debate over survival of the fetus which reduces to an issue of sexual pleasure or of private convenience, whether for physical or economic reasons. The scriptural view is that God gives life in the womb, and that one dehumanizes sex relationships by disjoining procreation and marriage and by treating intercourse as the mere momentary pleasure of two transitory partners.

What often complicates the issue of abortion are unfortunate pregnancies caused by incest or rape and fetuses subject to severe mental deformity. Seldom does birth of a baby any longer jeopardize the mother's actual survival; abortion is more frequently contemplated, therefore, in reference primarily to the mother's mental rather than physical condition. About four percent of all abortions occur at or beyond sixteen weeks of pregnancy, and hence in the second trimester; it is generally assumed that of this four percent at least three percent are performed because of severe life-depleting or life-threatening complications to either the fetus or the mother.

Where incest or rape is involved, one might argue for the legitimacy of abortion on the ground that God wills intercourse and conception within monogamous marriage, and that the aggrieved victim of assault should not in these circumstances be penalized by a violator's aggression. Authorities are often skeptical of a pregnancy attributed to rape, however, particularly if the indicated assault was not reported to police within 24 or 48 hours. Even here largely unexplored alternatives to abortion exist, however, including placement for adoption. When ecclesial agencies insist on preservation of fetal life under any and all circumstances, including that of severe physical deformities, should not such agencies be expected to share the otherwise crushing financial cost of sustaining life at the outer fringes of normalcy or abnormalcy?

Do therapeutic abortions differ in degrees of legitimacy? Where genetic deformity disallows mental and moral capacities identified with the *imago Dei*, does therapeutic abortion have greater justification than in cases of lesser deprivation? Some persons contend that the sanctity and dignity of full personhood belongs to every fetus — whatever its so-called quality — from the moment of conception, and that the biblical precedent of compassion towards the weak excludes abortion on any ground whatever. But even if therapeutic abortion should be allowable in cases of radical mental deformity, of incest and rape, and of actual threat to the mother's survival, no case could be made on moral grounds for destroying the at least 1,425,000 additional fetuses that comprise America's annual abortion statistics.

X

The passionate evangelical interest in the historical Jesus touches what is indispensable and central to genuine Christian belief. Apart from the fact of divine incarnation and Jesus Christ's sinlessness, substitutionary atonement and bodily resurrection, the foundations of Christian faith collapse. Critical reconstructions of the role of Jesus betray, even require, an altered view of God. This is as evident in David Friedrich Strauss' insistence that a thoroughly modern spirit must consider anachronistic interest in the Jesus of history[16] as in

---

[16]David Friedrich Strauss, *The Christ of Faith and the Jesus of History*, trans. and ed. by Leander E. Keck (Philadelphia: Fortress Press, 1977).

Rudolph Bultmann's disavowal of it as based on a misunderstanding of Christianity[17] and in Herbert Braun's view that the miraculous aspects of Jesus' life — from virgin birth to messiahship and ascension — merely attribute to the Nazarene legendary features borrowed from Hellenistic-oriental savior figures.[18]

Jesus bequeathed his followers no formal and schematic pattern of behavior. His messianic mission involved certain vocational commitments applicable only to him and to his own ministry. But he nonetheless left an example of self-denial, of unreserved trust in an obedience to the Father, and of a life ever and fully open to the Holy Spirit, that remains normative for Christians in all generations.

Yet we must not minimize the personal example of Jesus during His earthly ministry as critics skeptical of biblical history are prone to do. Both liberation theology and the theology of revolution would profit, for example, from attending to the fact that neither Jesus, nor the apostles He instructed, promoted revolutionary liberation from Rome. Jesus' high view of sexual morality is another case in point. While modern relativists often demean it as simply a cultural reflex of the Jewish heritage, they ignore the fact that the culture-conditionedness of ethics would also invalidate their own alternatives.

According to the New Testament, the Holy Spirit as an inner renewable divine resource is the wellspring of virtue and of the virtuous life. It would be hard to overstate the contrast of this view with that of the Greeks, especially Aristotle, and of the so-called "works religions" that connect salvation with human achievement rather than with divine grace. Aristotle taught that we attain the good life by harmoniously balancing our inner propensities, in short, by pursuing the "golden mean" that avoids extremes. But Christianity calls for death of the unregenerate nature and birth of a new nature by the Spirit of God, and

---

[17]Rudolph Bultmann, *Jesus Christ and Mythology* (New York: Charles Scribner's Sons, 1958).

[18]Herbert Braun, *Jesus of Nazareth: The Man and His Time*, trans. by Everett R. Kalin (Philadelphia: Fortress Press, 1979), p. 25.

not simply for a reshuffling of the old nature. In Jesus's words, "make the tree good and the fruit shall be good" (Matt. 12:33).

Since the resurrection of the Crucified One, the ascended Christ in and by the Spirit has been personally present in believers as a dynamic life-transforming power. Christian morality therefore has about it an element of buoyant Easter joy sustained by the Risen Jesus as our Eternal Contemporary. The regenerate believer does not live the Christian life autonomously "on his own," but he lives "in Christ" (Gal. 2:20) as one in whom Christ by the Spirit dwells and works. Christian morality is not merely conformity to a set of rules inferred from ethical principles, although the Risen Lord does in fact rule over the church in the world through the propositional teaching of the Bible; Christian morality participates also in the extension of divine sovereignty over the world through the Son's moral energizing of believers by the Spirit.

Whenever the New Testament speaks of the coming future restoration of the presently blemished divine image in man, it does so in terms of the believer's full conformity to the image of Jesus Christ (1 John 3:2; cf. Rom. 8:29, Col. 2:9). Where else in the history of human thought, we may ask, is the humanity God approves—both in earthly history and in eternity to come—so decisively and exclusively linked with the moral life and work of one person? While Jesus confidently confronted His foes with the question, "Which of you convinceth me of sin?" (John 8:48), those who knew Him best attested His sinlessness.

Anyone who has pursued doctoral studies in theology and/or philosophy knows how seldom the private life of founders of influential speculative systems and of great world religions is considered at all relevant, even when weighed by those systems or religions. Contemporary moralists write lengthy textbooks without a single reference to Jesus of Nazareth. Yet of whom can it be said as of the Nazarene that in Him the Word truly became flesh? Earlier generations asked whether Socrates might perhaps have been saved on the ground of a positive response to general divine revelation. But most present-day scholarship in ethics is so largely out of touch with the Gospels that it seldom any longer asks the core question of the New Testament: Is Jesus of Nazareth God's one and only Son, or is He a deceiver, a blasphemer? And in the latter event, what would it say for the nature of things if the noblest impulses of all the centuries and the most immaculate life in history were the fruit of deception?

XI

No emphasis finds profounder expression in Jesus' teaching than that on the kingdom of God. The Old Testament depicts God the Creator as King of the universe (Ps. 95:3–5) and regards the nations of this world (Ps. 22:8; Jer. 46:18) and their rulers (Dan. 2:37, 4:17, etc.) as under his jurisdiction. God is specially King of his covenant-people Israel (Deut. 33:5; 1 Sam. 12:12) to whom He promised and gave their land. But when Israel's earthly kings disregarded Him, God punished them and sent the Hebrews into captivity. The inspired prophets had given assurance of a future era of peace and righteousness in which Messiah would succeed to David's throne. This messianic vision exerted an enduring influence upon Hebrew expectations. During the inter-biblical period Jewish thought about the kingdom diversified into numerous strands, among them an emphasis on the individual's duty to submit to God's rule as stipulated by Mosaic law; nationalistic expectation of an earthly political kingdom which God would restore and over which God would rule while destroying Israel's oppressor nations; and anticipation that Messiah would as God's agent usher in a new era. Some writers more than others emphasized the kingdom's transcendent aspects above its earthly features. Others held out hope that the temple would be rebuilt; still others held that the righteous dead would be resurrected to share in the new age.

According to the Synoptic Gospels, what best summarizes the whole of Jesus' teaching is this theme of the kingdom or rule of God (Matt. 4:17; Mark 1:15; Luke 4:43). Jesus instructed His disciples to make it their main concern (Matt. 10:7; Luke 9:2).

Jesus focused not simply on God's transcendent eternal rule

(Matt. 24:34 f.), but also encouraged the view that His own earthly life and ministry constituted God's final redemptive act (Matt. 10:7; Luke 10:9 f.) and that the eschatological kingdom had already dawned in his own conquest of sin, death and Satan; He focused as well on a climactic future consummation when He the Son of Man would return in universal power and glory (Matt. 26:29). In the present interim God anticipatively extends His kingdom or rule as human beings participate individually in the kingdom through repentance and the new birth (John 3:3,5). Jesus' disciples constitute earth's new society; they are light and salt to the world, a regenerate *ecclesia* that the Risen Lord rules as living head of a body encompassing both believing Jews and Gentiles. His followers are to model a character and behavior exceeding that of Pharisees and scribes (Matt. 5:19 f.). While not itself the kingdom, the church is the kingdom's most vital approximation and manifestation in the present age. Its ongoing mission is to extend the King's victory over the hostile forces of sin and evil, injustice and oppression; this it does by proclaiming the Gospel, declaring and exemplifying the standards by which the King will judge mankind at his return, and witnessing to the present privileges and joys of serving the Risen Lord to whom all humanity must ultimately bow.

Jesus bids His disciples to pray daily (Matt. 6:10 ff.) for the kingdom to come. Its future blessings go beyond its manifestation both in Jesus' historical life and ministry and in the new character and virtues bestowed daily by the Risen Lord through the Holy Spirit (Rom. 14:17; Gal. 5:22). The Son of Man's second coming would be the occasion of the resurrection of the dead, the final judgment of humanity and of the nations, and the full conformity of all believers to the image of Jesus Christ.

This abbreviated reference to the kingdom of God will serve to illumine the impact of the Christian view of man in society upon subsequent Western thought. Until the present century it had been widely assumed, in view of biblical thought, that without divine regeneration sinful man could shape no historical utopia. Even Darwinians, although disdaining the doctrine of original sin, spoke guardedly of the perfectibility of man in view of supposed inherited brute impulses. But the biblical conviction of a final consummation of history in which good will surely prevail and evil is decisively conquered was metamorphosed into a secular doctrine of the kingdom, one unrelated to supernatural redemption and regeneration and linked instead to a supposed comprehensive law of evolutionary development. In the early part of our entry an optimistic doctrine of the latent or essential goodness of man and of inevitable progress to utopia thus came to capture the speculative loyalty of scholars who had actually broken with biblical realities and vitalities even while they mistakenly believed they had purified and elevated scriptural teaching.

It is remarkable how many modern social conceptualities are in fact secular reconstructions and mutations of biblical emphases. The communist notion of a future classless society in which the proletariat inherit the earth in a socialist utopia achieved by world revolution rests upon a perversion of basic biblical motifs. The transnational, transcultural and transracial church provides a kind of picture of the League of Nations and then of the United Nations; these structures obscure rather than illumine revealed religion, however, and cloud God's transcendent purpose through the pluralistic nations to which the Gospel is to be addressed. The modern vision of a warless world—in which nuclear energy is used only for peaceful purposes—has shallow roots in the biblical anticipation of an age when "swords will be beaten into plowshares" (Isa. 2:4).

Whatever its borrowed vocabulary or ideas, the modern view conspicuously suppresses the messianic component, that indispensable central ingredient of the biblical vision of the coming age of universal justice and peace. With its dark view of human sin and of humanity's spiritual dilemma, the Bible assesses the moral compromises and the overweaning self-interest of fallen human nature far more realistically than does the optimistic modern reading of man in society. The Bible recognizes the human need for a transformed character; it affirms the penitent sinner's access to redemptive reconciliation with God, and the genesis of a new nature in which God etches His law and will upon hearts dedicated to the love of God and His service; it finds the kingdom of God historically and anticipatively unveiled in the sinless life and resurrection of Messiah and reflected by the New Society over which Christ rules.

At the same time world history falls within the universal providence of God as an arena in which the many nations serve as the context for both unregenerate and regenerate life and in which civil government has a necessary though limited role. In this context self-interest is not necessarily inordinate, but is one of the survival-promoting features of human existence. The misuse of power and freedom calls for public control, but public control is also one of the ways by which power is misused. The Christian conviction that flawed man is by nature selfish will alert him against the expectation that any economic or political system can be perfect. But the biblical outlook will also prevent him from viewing private property and wealth as inherently demonic, rather than as an entrustment for service of God and man. The Bible encourages labor for reward as well as for survival and insists upon fair wages; it approves private property, albeit not in terms of absolute right but rather of stewardship. It provides no basis for acclaiming a controlled economy as superior to a free market, as though bureaucracy is endowed with omnipotence.

In summary, the moral fortunes of the West hinge both in the past and in the present upon the fate of the Bible and on appropriation or neglect of its spiritual and ethical realities. The sovereign, self-revealing, rational Creator is moving history toward a decisive moral denouement involving final judgment of both mankind and the nations. Speculative secular alternatives cannot vindicate objective morality and lead only to subjectivism and skepticism. The resources of revealed religion, including divine-command morality which the messianic Redeemer fulfilled in the spirit of obedient love, together with the dynamic transforming power of the Holy Spirit, have in the past rescued the West from paganism and channeled *agape* at high tide into an otherwise bleak history. The loss of biblical virtues and vitalities is the occasion of the moral confusion of our age, besieged as it now is by sensate, scientific and sexual priorities. Its revered scientific method of knowing cannot identify fixed truth and the good. Only renewed respect for God's commandments can confront the cardinal vices of idolatry, murder, adultery, covetousness and false witness that so conspicuously underlie modern social instability, and only renewed neighbor-love can defuse the many hostilities that plague community life. The Bible's pervasive regard for social justice enlivened by the bold witness of the prophets, its sure confidence in the invincibility of the dawning kingdom of God, and its motivating and sustaining power for personal and public righteousness can, by the truth and vitalities of the Gospel, bring to contemporary society the moral transformation it desperately needs.

The Fundamental Principles
of Biblical Ethics

Thomas J. Burke

Dr. Thomas J. Burke is presently a faculty member of Hillsdale College with teaching responsibilities in the philosophy of religion, historical theology, epistemology, and biblical studies. He earlier taught at the Sacred Heart School of Theology, Hales Corner, Wisconsin. Burke received his bachelor of arts degree from Baylor University and went on to earn the M.Div. from Trinity Evangelical Divinity School and his Ph.D. from Northwestern University. Dr. Burke has also earned a master's in philosophy from Michigan State University where he is in the final stages of completing his second doctorate. He is the editor of Volume 2 of *The Christian Vision: Man and Morality*.

The history of Western philosophy and theology has had a continuing, one might even say central, interest in ethical questions. By stressing metaphysical and epistemological theories, standard introductory courses in the history of philosophy actually distort the beginning student's view of that history, leading him to the erroneous opinion that philosophy is primarily an attempt to construct a cosmology and to define the limits or extent of man's cognitive powers.

In reality, the primary aim has more often been to develop an ethical system which would enable its adherents to know and do the Good, howsoever the latter is defined. Kant, for example, wrote his first critique, a massive and distressingly abstruse epistemological theory, only because he felt it imperative to discover the limits of human knowledge in general before he could establish a sound theory of ethical knowledge in particu-

25

lar. Hume's *Treatise of Human Nature* is usually thought of as a skeptical epistemological study. Actually, the major portion is devoted to ethical theory, the epistemology of Book I acting as a prolegomenon to the central and, together, larger Books II and III which attempt to apply the principles derived in Book I to the subject of morals. Spinoza entitled his major work *Ethics*, and Mill is most famous for his defense of utilitarianism. This is not to say, of course, that no philosophers have been interested in metaphysics and epistemology for their own sakes, but merely to point out that these concerns are not as dominant as a cursory look at philosophy in the West might lead one to believe.

Theology too is often thought of as primarily a study of speculative theories about the nature of God, with little practical application to even the religious life, to say nothing of ethics in the secular sphere. But again, the theological tradition has rarely and only waywardly been considered an end in itself. More usually and more properly it has been pursued and expounded as a necessary prelude to developing a competent understanding of the nature and will of God in order that one might worship Him correctly and behave in a way pleasing to Him. In other words, theology has been ultimately concerned with the task of constructing a satisfactory ethical and evaluational foundation for both religious and secular life.

Needless to say, the Bible has had an immense effect on the formal ethical theorizing of philosophers and theologians since the first few centuries of the Christian era. It has not, of course, been the only influence, but as long as it was considered the Word of God, its teaching on any topic even remotely connected with ethical matters needed to be taken into consideration. Moreover, the Bible has had a dominant effect upon the ethical beliefs and practices of the non-academician through the average person's association with the church and synagogue, priests, ministers, and rabbis, and the pervasive influence of religion throughout society. Indeed, it can safely be said that even in our supposed "secular age," the average person's ethical beliefs are largely a personally distilled understanding of the

Golden Rule mixed with common notions of justice, fairness, and compassion. The latter, it should be noticed, looms as large as it does primarily because of its dominant role in biblical ethics.

Given this history, a clarification of those notions which undergird or are foundational in the Bible *vis à vis* ethical questions and values would certainly help our understanding of Judeo-Christian ethics in general, enable us to more appropriately evaluate its viability, acceptability, and usability in the twentieth century, and aid in the development within the framework of that tradition of our own ethical views. Consequently, in this paper we shall attempt to identify and elaborate upon those principles which form the foundation for biblical ethics. That is, we shall attempt to delineate and explain those basic tenets in the Bible which are determinative of its ethical outlook, and which any and all ethical theorizing desiring to be a legitimate continuation of this tradition must take into consideration. For those working within the Judeo-Christian tradition, the importance of these principles cannot be overemphasized, for they form the ultimate criteria of both theoretical and practical ethical decisions.

The procedure followed in this paper will be to develop these principles in terms of polarities or, alternatively, complementarities. This will make it easier to show that apparent tensions and conflicts actually betoken underlying interdependencies. In fact, a proper understanding of biblical ethical principles can only be achieved if seen in tandem with their complements. Consequently, we shall elaborate these concepts by means of the following pairs: absolutism and teleology, holiness and love, freedom and responsibility, dignity and depravity, transcendence and immanence, society and the individual, and law and principle.

Absolutism and Teleology

The first polarity is between absolutism and teleology. Despite the philosophical objections which can and have been raised against grounding ethics in divinity, there can be no doubt that in the Old and New Testaments the reason certain acts, attitudes, and desires are considered wrong is because they are contrary to God's nature and consequent will for His creation. The Bible sees no tension between the universality of ethical principles and the will of God as expressed in His commands. To say that God is morally perfect was, given the rival conceptions of the day, to provide a new concept of divinity; but from the perspective of later Jewish and Christian faith, it became an analytic truth. If He were less, He would not be the God of Israel, and, consequently, any command He gives cannot conceivably be morally awry. God's moral perfection has neither cause, criteria, nor rival; rather, His nature is the "cause" of morality and His will the criterion by which the morality of all other rational, moral beings is to be judged. Since ethics is in this sense grounded in God's nature, it is as unchangeable as God Himself.

This does not exclude the possibility of moral conflict, of course. Indeed, God Himself seems on occasion to be faced with moral dilemmas, as, for example, in the stories of Noah and Job. In the former, God must decide whether to wipe out all of humanity or save a relatively, but not absolutely, righteous family knowing full well that their progeny will fare no better than those he is exterminating. In the latter, God is faced with the challenge of either allowing the real ethical motivations of Job to go untested, thereby leaving it dubious whether or not He really can have a truly loyal follower, or bringing tribulation to one who is completely unworthy of such treatment. Indeed, the entire drama of redemption as proclaimed in the New Testament is predicated upon the assumption that the Christ will suffer unjustly for the unjust in order that the unjust may be declared just, and that because God wills it so. Resolution without divine self-contradiction may be possible, but tension is nevertheless present. The underlying assumption, however, is that the judge of all the earth cannot but do right, and whatever the outcome, God will not be guilty of a felony against His own nature. If indeed God *is* morally perfect and if His morally perfect nature is the ground and criterion of morality, morality cannot be changeable, relativistic, or utilitarian.

Although morality in the Bible has a definite absolutist aspect, there is also a teleological one. God's nature is unchanging, but part of that nature is God's infinite love, and no being who can be characterized as love itself can simply disregard the effects certain actions will have on other sentient beings. At least part of the value equation will include the realization of those states of affairs which will bring those beings to a proper and satisfying consummation. Even a God whose only concern was the justness of His world would not be content to create beings with certain potentialities beneficial to themselves, others and the world in general, and then allow those potentialities to remain unrealized and those beings forever frustrated. Consequently, if indeed the God of the Bible is responsible for the present universe, He as well as we will value those things which are valuable to us and will consider it not only part of our, but also part of His ethical obligations to see that they are realized.

The biblical assumption of God's absolute moral perfection is so pervasive it hardly needs substantiation. God is "a God of truth and without iniquity, just and right is He" (Deut. 32:4). "The Lord is good" (Ps. 100:5), "Righteous art thou, O Lord, and upright are thy judgments" (Ps. 119:137), the Lord is He with whom there is "no variableness, neither shadow of turning" (James 1:17) and whose law is "the perfect law of liberty" (James 1:25). "He dwells in unapproachable light" (I Tim. 6:16), and indeed, "God is light, and in Him is no darkness at all" (I Jn. 1:4). His word is truth (Ps. 119:160), He alone is good (Lk. 18:19), and sin can be defined as the transgression of His law (I Jn. 3:4).

The Bible is just as emphatic, however, about God's concern for His creatures' welfare. The numerous beatitudes scattered throughout Scripture amply demonstrate that God has so cre-

ated man that adherence to God's just law and will will ultimately (Is. 32:20; Rev. 14:13) and inevitably yield "blessed-
ness," i.e., "happiness" (e.g., Matt. 5:3–11; Ps. 1:1, 32:1, 40:4,
41:1, 65:4). Consequently, "The statutes of the Lord are right,
rejoicing the heart" (Ps. 19:8), and "the judgments of the Lord
are true and righteous altogether" (Ps. 19:9), and, therefore,
"More to be desired are they than gold, yea, than much fine
gold: sweeter also than honey and the honeycomb" (Ps. 19:10).
The fulfillment of man's desires is most completely attained in
the enjoyment, one might even say, the thrill, of living according to the good and perfect will of this good and perfect God.
Note that in one breath Isaiah calls God both just and a savior
(Is. 45:21). God's moral perfection is most clearly displayed in
his salvific acts, acts which are designed to bring man from an
existence of grief, despair, and pain into one of inextinguishable
life, eternal hope, and unspeakable joy. When, in the book of
Revelation, St. John describes the glories of the New Heaven
and the New Earth, he pictures the God who alone is good as
wiping all tears from the eyes of His people. Moreover, "there
shall be no more death, neither sorrow, nor crying, neither shall
there be any more pain" (Rev. 21:4). Such language is not
intended to lull the flock into a pie-in-the-sky stupor which will
enable the rich and powerful to exploit their precious lives; it is
the necessary consummation of a world created and directed by
a God of absolute moral perfection. The God who can brook
no evil sent His Son into the world that men might have life and
might have it abundantly (Jn. 10:10). As Calvin wrote, God
rules both inwardly and outwardly "more for our own sake than
his."

There is, then, a balance between absolutism and teleology in
the biblical perspective on values, a balance which results from
the very nature of the God therein proposed. It is the all-
encompassing concern with God as the ground of ethics that
makes concern with His creatures, particularly sentient and
rational ones, factors which need to be considered in ethical
determinations. God's godhood implies a concern with the crea-

ture's creaturehood; theocentricity does not entail either "the-goticity" or "thegoicity." Indeed, it is their undoing. A god of maximal ethical purity cannot but concern himself with the concerns of other persons. In fact, in the Bible the ground for neighborly love is the sovereignty and centrality of God: Because His nature is the determinant of ethical goodness and because His nature is unmitigatingly centered on the needs of others, such concern is a paramount ethical consideration. It seems paradoxical, but the very centrality of God, the positing of "His glory" as the fundamental purpose of human life, demands an intense interest in the welfare of other creatures, human or not. Theocentricity does not undermine, but sustains *agape* and the teleological factor the latter inevitably introduces into ethical considerations.

Holiness and Love

The second polarity is closely related to the first. The absolut-ist dimension in ethics derives from God's holiness as the teleo-logical dimension derives from His love, and so our first com-plementarity is actually dependent upon the second. The very nature of God as perfect holiness and infinite love makes it necessary to balance absolutism and teleology, principles and ends, in any ethics based upon a Judeo-Christian understanding of the world. It is incumbent upon us, therefore, to investigate the relationship between these two attributes of God and the implications they pose for ethical reflection in a biblical perspective.

On the one hand, the Bible presents God as being of incom-parable holiness, unable to abide the least taint of moral lassi-tude, a God who is so uncompromising and unrelenting in his concern with moral impeccability that He pursues transgressors with unparalleled indignation. But on the very next page, He is presented as a God of infinite mercy and compassion who will-ingly sacrifices Himself for the sake not only of the downtrodden and weak, but the undeserving and wicked. Surely there is some inconsistency between an avenging God whose purity is a consuming fire and a God who comes as a suffering servant and commands His followers to turn the second cheek when an adversary strikes the first.

The inconsistency is only apparent, but simplistic resolutions which rely on superficial doctrines of the atonement miss the complementarity which an adequate doctrine of God's ethical nature requires. Most of the difficulty lies in primitive ideas of God's wrath and sentimental concepts of His love. Certainly, a god who is filled with petty egocentric pique at any and all upstaging of his divine personage is irreconcilable with a god who will lavish the most determined degenerate with repeated kindnesses and terms of endearment. While, on the one hand, such gods may resemble those of Hollywood's typical "uninformed fundamentalist" (of both Protestant and Catholic varieties), and, on the other hand, the liberally indoctrinated do-gooder, there is only superficial resemblance to the Deity revealed in Holy Writ.

The attribute of holiness emphasizes His unremitting concern with moral purity and absolute justice, but if divorced from His infinite compassion and mercy, it turns into a mechanical application of legalistic rules. The decision to be holy requisite for true holiness, to be just for true justice, can often only be made if the moral outlook of the decision-maker demands a moral choice between viable moral alternatives. If God were no more than a justice algorithm, such decision-making would be not only unnecessary, but also impossible. Holiness must be balanced by an equal regard for its seeming opposite, for a truly holy decision must involve both evaluating the needs and rights of all persons and the scrutiny of all relevant issues, not merely the legally prescribed punishment for a judicially inscribed trespass. Legality can be enacted with mathematical precision, required with military efficiency, and carried out with mechanical regularity; justice and holiness cannot.

Love, in its biblical meaning, it must similarly be observed, refers neither to sentimentality nor lawlessness. Indeed, as Leon

Morris has noted, mercy which is not balanced with justice ceases to be mercy.[1] If one bears no punishable guilt, justice, not compassion, demands release. Only those guilty and justly deserving of punishment are possible candidates for clemency and mercy. But mercy, compassion, forgiveness, and such like virtues are, in the biblical view, particular subclasses of love. We have experienced the forgiveness of sins, received the mercy of God, and beheld the compassion of the Almighty only because He has loved us. "But God commendeth His love toward us, in that, while we were yet sinners, Christ died for us" (Rom. 5:8). "But God, who is rich in mercy, for His great love wherewith He loved us, even when we were dead in sins, hath quickened us together with Christ . . ." (Eph. 2:4-5). All God has done for us has been done because of His love.

A moment's reflection makes it clear that this kind of love, the *agape* of which the Old and New Testament speak, is a love which operates as a moral principle; it is not a sort of interpersonal analogue to universal gravitation. Human desire and longing is indeed a type of love, and as such can be debasing or exalting depending upon the worthiness and fittingness of the object loved and the manner in which it is loved by the lover. Such can and has been called "love" by thinkers as important as Plato and St. Augustine and as diverse as St. Thomas and your favorite dime novelist. Consequently, its importance and its propriety cannot be gainsaid.

But the love which the New Testament extols and enjoins is a function of neither ontological status nor passion—either prosaic or sublime. It is a moral consideration which considers neither the worthiness of a fitting recipient, the profit to be gained from such benevolent action, nor the appropriate response to be expected from a properly grateful beneficiary. Like holiness, love is concerned with all aspects of a moral situation, but unlike holiness, it values needs as opposed to

---

[1]Leon Morris, *The Cross in the New Testament* (Grand Rapids: Eerdmans Publishing Company, 1965), p. 386.

rights. The Bible encourages neither inflexibility nor softness. It does, however, require both justice and love. Paul's oft-quoted statement, "Love is the fulfillment of the law," ought to make it clear that love is antithetical to neither justice nor legality. Rather, the *agape* of the New Testament is the epitome of moral behavior because its concern for needs does not extinguish concern for rights, but exists in symbiotic relationship with the latter.

Freedom and Responsibility

A third polarity is that between freedom and responsibility. The biblical notion of freedom is rooted in the concept of God's Image in man. His cognitive, rational, personal and moral abilities transcend those of all other creatures made from the dust of the earth. Man is able to mirror and thereby glorify God's own nature and, consequently, unlike any other creature has the ability to make rational and moral choices. Such decisions, obviously, demand the ability to act from oneself, to will. It is plain that if such an ability is realized, those who possess it are then responsible for their decisions. Freedom without responsibility is not merely license, it is unintelligible. When this freedom is considered the result of a divinely instituted capacity whose purpose was to allow its recipients the privilege to reflect the glorious nature of their infinite and perfect creator, the responsibility not only arises from subsequent relationships to other entities, but more immediately from one's relationship to his or her Creator.

Moreover, this freedom has, then, a positive aim to fulfill, for it was bestowed with an intention and cannot be construed as if that intention never existed. Consequently, the maximization of individual freedom becomes a moral imperative because only in conditions of freedom can human beings be what they were intended to be, morally responsible creatures whose moral behavior does more than simply obey moral imperatives; that very obedience itself allows humans to transcend their own limited existence and participate in the divine. Assuredly, all men are men, but only free men are able to properly fulfill the divine intention. Insofar as men are bound by illegitimate restrictions on their intellectual, political, economic, and social actions, their ability to be what they ought to be and to do what they ought to do is impeded, and the tighter the restrictions, the greater the disrespect to God and the less the capability of such men to honor and glorify the One whose glory and honor they were to manifest and magnify.

It is clear, of course, that from the biblical perspective, freedom is not an unrestricted right, but a means to responsible behavior, a necessary prerequisite to moral action. It is a privilege which enables its possessors to be morally responsible beings. Plainly, freedom without responsibility is as unthinkable and outrageous as responsibility without freedom.

Dignity and Depravity

A fourth polarity lies in the necessary balance between dignity and depravity. Given the transcendent purpose which the Bible envisons as man's birthright, he must be seen as "a little lower than the angels" (Ps. 8:5), but designed to become those whom the latter were created to serve (Heb. 1:14). Created in the Image of God, man's unique relationship to his Creator and unsurpassed place in the divine plan were reaffirmed, indeed, elevated beyond all conceivable expectation, by the incarnation. The Word became flesh, the Son of God the Son of man, and the hypostatic union of God the Son with man, the pinnacle of God's creation, has revealed the greatness and worth God has bestowed upon him. The Bible places man in a class by himself, a class which imparts to him rights, privileges and responsibilities, i.e., which make him a moral being. As the bearer of God's Image, he takes his place along with God as a being whose treatment and activity is subject to moral criteria. Respect, honor, politeness, and other such amenities are, on this view, moral responsibilities because they derive from the basic dignity of man which, in turn, derives from his possession of the divine Image. Likewise, man's responsibility and respectful treatment of himself and others, the keeping of one's word, the care of one's person, and all other such traditional virtues are merely the effective implacement of due regard for man's dignity as the bearer of God's Image.

On the other hand, the Bible also recognizes the abject state of man at present. As far above the rest of creation as he is by virtue of God's Image, due to his plunge into the depths of depravity through willful disobedience to the will of God and non-conformity to the nature of God, he is now equally far from being the noble and righteous being his author intended. In the Bible, man is viewed as presently, although not essentially, a sinner. "Sin" is a word which has come to be associated with an out-of-date pietism, inapplicable in our enlightened era where we know that all behavior has physiological, psychological, and sociological determinants, where things are never black and white, guilt is outmoded, punishment immoral, and rehabilitation and perhaps the protection of society the only valid justifications for a penal system. Real responsibility and the corresponding punitive action are ruled out of court. "Sinner," then, becomes a designation with no designees, a name with no referent.

But despite the apparent humaneness of such a view, it is actually destructive of humaneness, for it denigrates man by viewing him as a mere vent in the total causal nexus we call the universe. His actions become reflexes, his decisions responses, his ideas mere imaginings, his knowledge simply hypotheses, and his personhood nature's advanced computer technology. His metaphysical stature as a spiritual being capable of knowing and relating to God is exchanged for the pottage of a materialistic organic soup. Morality becomes convention, ethics prudence, and education behavior modification and indoctrination. What purports to "elevate" man in reality eliminates him, and he takes his place with the other playthings of the universe. If man is to retain dignity, he must also retain guilt for his wrong doings, i.e., he must be open to the frightful possibility of finding himself a sinner, one who knowingly, willfully, and guiltily transgresses the moral law of God, thus becoming liable to rejection and punishment by that God.

Not surprisingly, this is exactly how the Bible sees man, and any Christian ethical reflection must regard him as such, recognizing that in his present state, the Image of God in man is distorted and disfigured. Thought on how man ought to behave and act must, in other words, take into consideration the actual nature of man as it is, realizing that current moral choices take place in a context of sin, a context which obscures the clarity of moral truth and creates ambiguities and morally impossible situations in which the moral thing is nevertheless not a satisfying thing.

Transcendence and Immanence

The biblical view of man fits smoothly into neither the sharp dualism of a Plato or a Descartes nor the materialism of a Lucretius nor the identity theory of a J. J. C. Smart. Man is a full-fledged member of both the material world and the heavenly city. His rightful place is in neither a world devoid of spirit or a heaven devoid of flesh, and so the biblical vision of utopia is a New Jerusalem which is as physical as the old but transformed by the full and unmitigated presence and reign of the King of Heaven. The ultimate vision for the individual is not a spiritual playground where blithe and contented spirits flutter hither and yon or a motionless nirvana where the only activity is the constant contemplation of the Deity. Instead, the Bible portrays the future Kingdom of God as populated with the same individuals who have traversed our present clime, but refurbished with a resurrection body like unto the Messiah's.

What makes the Kingdom of Heaven the Kingdom of Heaven is the uninhibited freedom these resurrected men possess to live under the unopposed rule of God. The New Heaven and the New Earth are what one might call a real down-to-earth place with real flesh-and-blood human beings. The future Kingdom is a continuation of this era, albeit purged of evil and sorrow and transformed into a city of glory and light. In Scripture, the duality between heaven and earth is as much a temporal duality between the present age and the coming age as it is a spacial duality between a non-physical heaven and a physical earth. It should be noted, however, that contrary to our present "theologeist," both are integral to the biblical understanding of man and the world.

What this implies for ethical reflection, however, is that one must consider seriously both aspects of man's citizenship, both parts of his fundamental nature, both stages in his history. The present and earthly cannot be either ignored or denigrated, but neither can the future or heavenly be forgotten or disparaged. Consequently, one finds in Scripture both a fervid concern with deeds done in this life and constant reminders that this present age is temporary and transient, soon to pass away, and, therefore, not a good long-term investment. Jesus exhorts his disciples to fear not him who can hurt the body, but only God who can destroy both body and soul (Matt. 10:28); St. Paul reminds his fellow Roman Christians that the pains of this present life are not worth comparing with "the glory which shall be revealed in us" (Rom. 8:18); and St. Peter is clear that believers are strangers and sojourners who have a home and resting place elsewhere and, therefore, need not be overly concerned with their present state, whether good or ill.

At first blush, this may seem odd, if not inconsistent. If indeed this life shall be transcended and, therefore, does not have ultimate value, why be concerned at all with what transpires here? Historically, the antinomian and ascetic implications of such questions have been pursued, but it is noteworthy that they are both faced and rejected in Scripture itself. It is not only because God is Creator that one ought to act in this world and treat its furniture, both organic and inorganic, in a responsible way, but also because of the intricate relationship between both heaven and earth, the present and the future. What transpires on earth in the present age is as important in the heavens as what occurs in the latter is vital for the former. Ethical choices, consequently, must take into consideration not only this life, but also the next; and, it must be added, not only the next, but this also.

The relationship is not perfectly symmetrical, of course. If a choice between the two is unavoidable, the temporal must give way to the eternal. But more often, the two spheres and their corresponding interests are seen as complementary rather than contradictory. Two examples of this are the biblical exoneration of capital punishment and the biblical espousal of extra-marital chastity. I know of no non-theistic moral justification for either that is unanswerable. Certainly, deterrence can be more humanely achieved by some means other than capital punishment, and any psychological damage resulting from promiscuity can be treated and reasonably well repaired. Some, of course, might simply feel it is worth the price.

In regard to the former, if the end of this life is the end of life, then it would seem that any view of justice which could sustain the justice of capital punishment would be outweighed by the fact that killing the guilty party will (1) not bring back the victim, and (2) not be of much help to the now deceased perpetrator. But this reasoning is less cogent when the existence of the guilty is not seen as coextensive with his physical life. If indeed man has a future life, if the cessation of his present physical life can have some benefit for him as well as others, then the imposition of strict justice might be justified.

In regard to the second, only if the marriage relationship is sacralized as a means of reflecting and imaging the love of God Himself can the preservation of one's sexual integrity in all other situations be seen as virtuous. That is, without the transcendent justification, chastity seems less a virtue than a superstition; given the imput of transcendent values, it can perform a moral as well as a clinical service.

These are not the only "traditional values" which are helped by, if not necessitating, a transcendent perspective, but they are examples which point out the importance of transcendence, i.e., of a theistic framework — not merely a dualistic one — for the maintenance of many values which have been traditionally accepted as ethical values. But it should be noted that the transcendent rationale works not by devaluing, but by imparting value to the temporal or immanent. Indeed, the temporal actually becomes more important and more value laden when seen as ultimately serving not merely its own interests, but more importantly also the interests of a transcendent realm. The theistic postulate, in addition to adding to our store of values, also gives to that store an importance and urgency which it otherwise lacks.

Society and the Individual

A sixth complementarity exists between the value of the individual and the claims of society. Because man has been created in God's Image, his individual worth derives not from his utility in the world or even to God, but from his nature as a being in God's Image. Because he is a free, responsible, rational person capable of true interpersonal communion with God and his fellow humans and of mirroring in those relationships and in his own mind and heart the very glory and goodness of the Lord, he can never be treated as a mere means to an end. This does not mean, of course, there are no ends superior in value to man, that man is the measure of all things; but it does mean that even when ends with greater intrinsic worth are involved, the individual cannot be dealt with as if he were non-human, sub-human, or inhuman. Each life, each soul—to use the biblical term—has "infinite" intrinsic value and, therefore, his treatment always creates a moral decisional situation.

This evaluation of man's ethical value is reflected in the biblical doctrines of responsibility and redemption. In Ezekiel the individual responsibility for sin is clearly spelled out (Ezk. 18). David laments and bewails his personal transgression against God in the adulterous liaison with Bathsheba (Ps. 51); the gospel calls all humans to repent of their own sins (Acts 2:38); and each individual will have to give account of himself on the day of judgment (II Cor. 5:10). Just as individualistic is the aim and offer of salvation. God loves each person in particular; Christ dies for each individual person; the Spirit indwells every believer, offering individual guidance, instruction and reproof; and the individual as well as the community is the object of God's electing, sanctifying, and glorifying grace. Thus, it is clear that if, on the biblical view, God so respects the individual's freedom and life that each person becomes both responsible to God and a possible object of His redemptive purposes, any ethics which pretends to take the Bible seriously must also take the individual as an irreducible moral factor.

But the value of the individual is, in Scripture, balanced by an equal concern for society and for humankind as a species. The Image of God in man has a social as well as an individual dimension, and a view of ethics which sees mankind as a mere collection of isolated, atomic elements having no natural or intrinsic relationships with each other drastically misses the biblical position. Israel's election is a corporate election as the people of God, and God visits the iniquity of the fathers upon the children to the third and fourth generation (Ex. 20:5); the believer is elected in Christ who is the head of the Church universal, and as staunch an individualist as Calvin holds that one comes into Christ only by way of that Church; the Christian has definite ethical obligations to his brothers and sisters in Christ; and the life eternal will take place in the context of a kingdom with a royal city, the new Jerusalem (Rev. 21:2). Man, in other words, is always part of a community of men and cannot remove himself from the problems, cares, concerns, and aspirations of that community. This holds not only for his social existence, but especially for his religious life. While the individual can and ought to approach God as an individual, offering his own petitions and thanksgivings, he cannot rightly limit himself to such worship. Worship is a corporate endeavor, and the saints worship the Lord of Hosts as a unified body of synchronized worshippers. The Bible does not extol or encourage hermit Christians, and the lone pilgrim worshipping his God in the wilderness bereft of all other human companionship might be congenial to Walden Pond, but not to the faith of Paul and Silas. Paul did not convert individuals, he built churches and envisioned the apostolic task as creating a holy temple in which each believer is a building stone.

Law and Principle

The final complementarity we shall discuss is that between law and principle. As noted earlier, on the one hand, sin is defined in the Bible as transgression of the law, and on the other hand, love can be called the fulfilling of the law. But the question immediately arises, which really defines the nature of biblical ethics? Is one to follow legal rules or find in some ethical concept such as love a universal principle by which all ethical decisions are to be determined and evaluated? At one place, the Bible praises the law as eternally set in the heavens, ever unchangeable as God Himself, and a sure guide for man's footsteps to follow if he would do the good (Ps. 119:89 ff.). In another place, Jesus invokes the welfare of man and the goodness of God to justify the breaking of Sabbath legislation, apparently asserting the rights of ethical principle over law (Mk. 2:23–28).

But the Bible knows no such conflict. The Paul who uttered the seemingly revolutionary phrase, "Love is the fulfilling of the law" (Rom. 13:10), warns his followers that willful and continued disobedience of definite commandments excludes one from the promises of the Kingdom (Eph. 5:19–21). As counter-intuitive as it may seem, each actually requires the other. Without principles such as love, law devolves into legalism and right behavior into blind obedience. But likewise, without law, love has no content and is without any clear meaning in certain situations. That is, what it means to love in a particular context will be ambiguous, and a loving decision will become subject to the vagaries of human emotions and the instability of human feelings. Law gives principles content and principles make law meaningful; one cannot long survive without the other. Consequently, biblical ethics can never be mechanical, the regular and unchanging application of rules to changing situations which necessarily leads to the inscrutable confusion of a casuistic labyrinth.

This entails the unsettling conclusion that one cannot simply either miraculously intuit the moral thing to do nor mathematically deduce it from a list of rules and a hierarchical ordering for those occasions when the rules conflict. Not only do all such rules come up against situations in which the morality requires that one or another of them be broken, but any hierarchical ordering will also come up against apparent exceptions. Perhaps Isabella in Shakespeare's *Measure for Measure* ought to sleep with Angelo to rescue her brother from almost certain death — or perhaps not. But regardless, the decision cannot be made by simplistically referring to an ordered list of rules, e.g., life is more important than chastity or, conversely, chastity is more important than physical life. Good reasons can be given for either choice if biblical values are appealed to. But will those who opt for chastity do so if the party to be saved holds the key to advances in medicine which will save innumerable lives, and if he is innocent to boot? If these conditions are not strong enough to make one waver, we can always make them stronger until continued choice of chastity over life would indicate either mental deficiency or a very immoral concern for one's own piety over the vital interests and needs of others.

In the same manner, one can modify the situation so that those who would naturally choose life over chastity would eventually change their minds about the moral priority in those circumstances. Suppose, for example, the hostage were Adolf Hitler circa 1938, and Isabella a time traveller from the 1950s whose parents were victims at Auschwitz? Far fetched, perhaps, but more realistic scenarios could easily be constructed. The point is that mechanistic application of rules is simply not possible in all situations. This does not entail that morality is relativistic, but that the absoluteness of the Good cannot be determined by a procedure which does not require the application of transcendent reason, i.e., reason which in principle cannot be duplicated by a computer.

At this point, it should be added that referral to man's proper end will not provide a simple solution in all cases either, for it is characteristic of a true moral dilemma that it calls into question just that very notion. What, in this circumstance, is the proper end of man? And, given we can determine that, which course of action open to one will best achieve that end?

It is this balance between law and principle which causes this distressing, if thoroughly human, situation. For this reason, Jesus not only deepens the meaning and understanding of law, but resorts to illustrating moral action through parables where one would rather have a clear and unambiguous command. In the end, good and right moral decisions can only come from good and righteous humans who act not only out of a good will, but also out of a good mind and a good heart. Consequently, it is not surprising that part of God's redemptive plan is the transformation of the human mind and heart so that God's people will again be fully in the Image and likeness of God and thereby enabled to act in a truly holy and loving manner. Their acts will proceed from their being. As St. Paul writes, "Be renewed in the spirit of your mind; and . . . put on the new man, which after God is created in righteousness and true holiness" (Eph. 4:23–24). Or again, "Be ye transformed by the renewing of your mind, that ye may prove what is that good, and acceptable, and perfect, will of God" (Rom. 12:2).

Two conclusions would seem to follow from the view of biblical ethics outlined above. First, biblical theistic ethics will differ from non-theistic and, at least at times, non-biblical theistic ethics in two ways. (1) The values accepted will differ, biblical theism considering certain behavior ethical which other systems will not and rejecting other behavior as unethical which others will find either acceptable or not morally unacceptable. (2) The rationale for ethical behavior from the biblical perspective will often be radically different than that of non-biblically based systems even when the behavior enjoined or rejected is the same.

Second, in the biblical view, ethical behavior is neither simplistic nor impossible. As an essentially personal dimension of life, it is characteristic only of rational beings. Consequently, it requires a type of reasoning and willing which cannot be reduced to mechanism or any other system adequate only to the purely physical realm.

The Existentialist Challenge to Christian Values: Sheer Freedom or Shaped Faith?

John S. Reist, Jr.

The Reverend John S. Reist, Jr. joined the faculty of Hillsdale College in 1985 as Professor of Christian Studies and Literature. Dr. Reist earned a B.A. in English literature from Houghton College, a master of divinity from Northern Baptist Theological Seminary, and his M.A. and Ph.D. in theology and literature from the University of Chicago. Previously he taught at Central Baptist Theological Seminary in Kansas City, Kansas; Ottawa University in Kansas City, Missouri; St. Paul School of Theology, Kansas City, Missouri; the Unity School; North Central College; College of Dupage; and Judson College. He is an ordained minister of the American Baptist Convention and an associate elder of the Northern Illinois Conference of the United Methodist Church. His articles, essays, and reviews have appeared in such journals as the *Journal of Religion, Anglican Theology Review, Christianity and Literature*, and *Christian Scholar's Review*.

Introduction: Terminal Terminology?

Anxiety. Estrangement. Abyss. Absurd. Ennui. Alienation. Facticity. Responsibility. Dread. Anomie. Anguish.

Geworfenheit. Zuhandenheit. Uebermensch. Entwurf. Dasein. Sorge. Befindlichkeit. Vorhandenheit. Schuld.

Mauvaise foi. Engagement. Mesure. L'homme révolté. Pour-soi. En-soi. Disponibilité. Nausée.

Man is a useless passion (Sartre). Resistance is impossible (Ivan Ilych). There is only one truly serious philosophical problem, and that is suicide (Camus). The infinite qualitative distinction between time and eternity (Barth and Kierkegaard). God is dead (Nietzsche). Hell is other people (Sartre). The teleological suspension of the ethical (Kierkegaard). I respectfully return God the ticket (Ivan Karamazov). Man is doomed to be free (Sartre). The benign indifference of the universe (Meursault). The heart has reasons that reason cannot know (Pascal).

All of the above terms and references come from that great cloud of modern witnesses known collectively as "existentialists"; to the average person who pays the rent and mows the lawn, they are confusing, perhaps even frightening, and it is not only that some of them are foreign and therefore unknown. It is also that even the English terms are so baffling that discussion is usually avoided or terminated by the average person — the same person who nonetheless cares enough to know a safety blitz from a suicide blitz, and an IRS 1040 from an IRS 1040A. Even more significantly, this potpourri of existential language suggests, when it does not openly declare, that there are no "average" men and women but estranged individuals, that humanity is radically lost or ill, that the universe merely turned up or accidently appeared, that God is dead, and that life itself is a terminal illness.

Karl Barth, probably the greatest theologian of this century, when telling of his reading during his retirement, stated that he was ". . . often overcome by big yawns when I listen to the endless prattle of the existentialists. . . ."[1] Yet Barth himself was early influenced by Kierkegaard, the great Christian existentialist, and his own discussion of Heidegger and Sartre in *Church Dogmatics* is a devastating critique which concludes that con-

---

[1] Jurgen Fangmeier and Hinrich Stoevesandt, eds., *Karl Barth: Letters 1961-68*, trans. by Geoffrey W. Bromily (Grand Rapids: William B. Eerdmans Publishing Co., 1981), p. 59.

temporary existentialism is ". . . a false alarm."[2] Nonetheless, existentialism (along with process thought) constitutes a great challenge or opportunity for Western Christian life and thought; were it not so, the subject would not appear for address and analysis in our CCA this fall.

The terminology of existentialism is not terminal; careful study of it and personal appropriation or rejection of it produce a sharpened awareness of the issues, principles, and values to which we must finally hold and which we must personally embody and demonstrate in our private and public moral life. However, I will argue that existentialism, as such, is essentially a terminal illness.

Despite its radical protest against the excesses of modern technology and industry, against herd morality and metaphysical abstractionism; and in spite of its occasional illuminating insight into the human condition, its outlook is debatable as an option for humanity. For, although it paints a graphic and poignant picture of the metaphysical, psychological, and ethical wounds modern man has suffered, existentialism wrongly frames the picture by ignoring reason and insisting on extreme passion and subjectivity, and thus isolates the picture from the transcendent God who, as the master painter, sustains us all.

In Search of a Title: "Alone in a Dreadful Wood"

I believe the title of my paper is the only one of the CCA presentations that indicates something is fearfully awry in our world: that our received Christian faith, tradition, and values might need some recasting; and that existentialism provides just such a strong encounter—either a threatening challenge or a constructive alternative. The other titles seem to support or require exegesis and exposition of biblical and theological val-

---

2 Karl Barth, *Church Dogmatics*, III/3, ed. by G. W. Bromily and T. F. Torrance (Edinburgh: T. & T. Clark, 1960), p. 349.

ues that are true and vivifying; that is, we should and must live by them. My paper is an "existential challenge" to all of this.

As I reflected on the implications of the title, especially of the word "challenge," I immediately and then continuously thought of the great opening scene of *Hamlet*, whose confused and estranged college student-hero, Hamlet, has been called home from school, not because his grades are down this term, but because he no longer has the home he remembers to which he might return. Young and inexperienced, but deep in vision and wild with longing, homeless Hamlet has long been taken to symbolize modern man, cut off from his sources, estranged from society (even from his beloved Ophelia), and unable to cope with the demands placed on him.

Shakespeare, master not only of character development and dramatic denouement, but also of ambience and setting, sets the stage from the beginning. The play opens with a challenge from Bernardo, "Who's there?", which seems natural enough since we are watching the changing of the castle guard just before sunrise. However, it is the entering, *relieving* guard who challenges, and immediately we sense that something is deeply wrong. The tired and frightened Francisco, who should have challenged, retorts, "Nay, answer me." And he then says, "For this relief much thanks. 'Tis bitter cold and I am sick at heart." Horatio, the scholar (read college professor) shows up and confidently assures them about the ghost, "Tush, tush, 'twill not appear"; and, of course, almost immediately, the ghost of Hamlet's father enters.

Into the midst of all this anxiety, dread, and confusion modern man—homeless humanity—in the guise of Hamlet is called to *act*, not just think, reflect, hold conferences, or publish papers as Horatio does. Act I ends with Hamlet's lamentation which is echoed throughout the ensuing centuries by such thinkers as Kierkegaard, Pascal, Schopenhauer, Nietzsche, Sartre, Heidegger, Unamuno, Camus and others:

> The time is out of joint;—O cursed spite,
> That ever I was born to set it right!

Contemporary life, then, is a challenge in which the wrong people appear; the people who do appear say the wrong things; the intellectuals are confused and helpless; and the current generation is seeking the lost tradition and values which nurtured their ancestors. Thus our CCA might be entitled: "Hamlet and Horatio at Hillsdale: The Bible and Traditional Western Values"!!

This challenge, "Who's there?", is real, both ethically and metaphysically. In his great modern poem, "For the Time Being: A Christmas Oratorio," W. H. Auden has the chorus chant:

> Alone, alone, about a dreadful wood
> Of conscious evil runs a lost mankind,
> Dreading to find its Father lest it find
> The Goodness it has dreaded is not good;
> Alone, alone, about our dreadful wood.[3]

That aloneness that causes us to dread both Transcendence and lost Transcendence is defined succinctly by the etymology of the word, "existentialism," which is derived from the Latin, *ex* (out of, from) plus *sistere* (to stand, to be located). Thus, to exist, existentialists insist, is to be distinct from all that one is not, in such a way that separation degenerates immediately into alienation and individuality deteriorates into isolation. This isolation is radical and extreme—from God, from fellow humanity, from history, and from the world of things. Coming to consciousness is also to fall from essence into existence, to be separated from one's nature. Paul Tillich has stated, ". . . existence is not united with essence; . . . Whatever exists, that is, 'stands out' of mere potentiality, is more than it is in the state of mere potentiality and less than it could be in the power of its essential nature."[4]

However, there are two kinds of existentialists—Christian (or

---

3 Edward Mendelson, ed., *W. H. Auden: Collected Poems* (New York: Random House, 1976), p. 273.

4 Paul Tillich, *Systematic Theology*, Vol. I (Chicago: University of Chicago Press, 1959), p. 203.

theistic) and non-Christian (or atheistic). Thus, the existential challenge to Christian values is both a family quarrel raised by Kierkegaard, Buber, Marcel and other Judeo-Christian existentialists, and also an assault from without the castle by such men as Heidegger, Sartre, Camus, and Nietzsche. With Hegel primarily in mind, Kierkegaard has said of traditional Christian metaphysicians and systematic theologians:

> In relation to their systems most systematizers are like a man who builds an enormous castle and lives in a shack close by; they do not live in their own enormous systematic buildings. . . . Spiritually speaking a man's thought must be the building in which he lives — otherwise everything is topsy-turvy.[5]

And Sartre, the atheist, has forcefully declared:

> Existentialism is nothing else than an attempt to draw all the consequences of a coherent atheistic position. . . . Existentialism isn't so atheistic that it wears itself out showing that God doesn't exist. Rather, it declares that even if God did exist, that would change nothing. There you've got our point of view. Not that we believe that God exists, but we think that the problem of His existence is not the issue.[6]

Whether the quarrel and the assault become an endless, ongoing siege or a critical confrontation in which fundamental issues are decided, this challenge to Christian values will not go away. Living in a dreadful wood, or a castle, or a shack, or a family, or a college dorm must be authentic; it must not avoid the existential challenge, nor may it ignore traditional Christian values.

The final terms of my title are "Christian values." What is the value of any thing, or any act? What is it worth? How is its

---

5 Sören Kierkegaard, *Journals*, in *Existentialism*, ed. by Robert C. Solomon (New York: Modern Library, 1974), p. 8.

6 "Existentialism," in *The Great Ideas Today, 1963* (Chicago: Encyclopaedia Britannica, Inc., 1963), p. 461.

worth determined, by its intrinsic nature or by its utility? By what authority does one decide that "authenticity" — a favorite word of existentialism — is valuable? The value of any thing, it seems to me, is what it costs. Henry David Thoreau remarked, ". . . the cost of a thing is the amount of what I will call life which is required to be exchanged for it, immediately or in the long run."[7] This has both a biblical and existential ring — "For what will it profit a man if he gains the whole world and forfeits his life? Or what shall a man give in return for his life?" (Matt. 16:26). Are there values which, when accumulated and arranged over the centuries into a system, offer us enduring principles based on truth by which to act? And what is the relation of such systems to God? In *In Memoriam*, Alfred Lord Tennyson, searching desperately for consolation following the death of his young friend, Arthur Hallam, wrote:

> Our little systems have their day;
> They have their day and cease to be:
> They are but broken lights of thee,
> And thou, O Lord, art more than they.[8]

If our systems of value are transitory and fragmented, does that mean that God, the source of our Judeo-Christian values, cannot be known, and therefore can never be obeyed in an *informed* manner? Tennyson further declared, following Kant:

> We have but faith: we cannot know;
> For knowledge is of things we see;
> And yet we trust it comes from thee,
> A beam in darkness: let it grow.[9]

Think of Kierkegaard's Abraham who, contrary to the received value that fathers should love and therefore not kill

---

[7] Henry David Thoreau, *Walden* (New York: Harper & Row, 1965), p. 23.

[8] Alfred Lord Tennyson, *In Memorium*, ed. by H. M. Percival (London: McMillan & Co. Ltd., 1955), p. 1.

[9] *Ibid.*, p. 2.

their sons, nevertheless takes Isaac up the hill, determined to obey the voice he has heard. In order to obey God, Abraham had to "teleologically suspend the ethical";[10] that is, what under normal conditions is a value — the life of one's son, Isaac — becomes bracketed in order to do the one thing needful — obey God.

Further, think of Jesus and the rich young man (read: enthusiastic college student): he has kept the commandments from his youth up; he knows his values; he is informed; his father has not taken *him* up the mountainside. Indeed, in response to the youth's question, "Good Teacher, what shall I do to inherit eternal life?" (Luke 18:18), Jesus, acknowledging the young man's value system since Jesus himself was the perfect embodiment of the Law, quotes several of the Ten Commandments, including "Honor your father and mother" (Luke 18:20). Yet, after the young man refuses Christ's command to sell everything he has in order to follow this "Good Teacher," the disciples declare, "We have left our homes and followed you" (Luke 18:28). And then Jesus responds (Luke 18:29–30): "Truly I say to you, there is no man who has left house or wife or brothers or parents or children, for the sake of the kingdom of God, who will not receive manifold more in this time, and in the age to come eternal life." How can Jesus command on the one hand, "Honor your father and mother," and on the other hand, commend the disciples for having left their homes and parents to be with him? Who is informed — Abraham, Jesus, the disciples, or the rich young man?

God, we are told, provided for Abraham. When Isaac asks in filial loyalty, "Where is the sacrifice?", Abraham replies "God will provide." Would he have provided for the rich young man? Are Judeo-Christian principles only conventional human moral duties, or are they revelatory of the will of God? Are values objective or subjective, personal or tribal, permanent or situational? If John Ruskin was right when he wrote, "For truly, the

---

[10]Sören Kierkegaard, *Fear and Trembling and the Sickness unto Death* (Garden City: Doubleday and Company, Inc., 1954), p. 77.

man who does not know when to die, does not know how to live,"[11] then certainly existentialists are right when they satirize and condemn conventional and nominal moral existence as not moral at all.

Are there distinctly Judeo-Christian values whose source is in the revelation of the will of God found in scripture, or are such values congruent with general human values present to all humanity because of the image of God (*imago Dei*) which—although sullied by sin—we all possess? Are there universal ethical principles known by reason, such as the four cardinal virtues of prudence, justice, temperance, and fortitude? If so, what is the relationship of those four to the three theological virtues—faith (the act by which we believe the "faith"—the things we do believe); hope (that by which the will is moved to act into the future, what the atheistic existentialists call "projection"); and love (the power by which the will is transformed and in-formed)? And, finally, what of the three counsels of perfection—poverty, chastity, and obedience? Are they only for the inner group—the monks and pastors, the mayors and professors? Or are they for all to undertake?

Thoreau has written: "There are nowadays professors of philosophy, but not philosophers."[12] These ten ethical categories come, of course, from the Roman Catholic ethical tradition as worked out by St. Thomas Aquinas and Thomists who followed him. They combine Aristotelian and Ciceronian categories with biblical foundations; but they have been radically criticized by such thinkers as Luther, Calvin, Kierkegaard, and Bonhoeffer. Abraham and the rich young man were men (*vir*); and virtue comes from *vir* which means manliness, strength, ability—perhaps we might say, "the right stuff." But Christian and non-Christian existentialists challenge this view that man has a nature, that humanity has an objective tradition of moral

---

[11]John Ruskin, "The Roots of Honor," in *Selections and Essays*, ed. by Frederick William Roe (New York: Charles Scribner's Sons, 1918), p. 324.

[12]*Walden*, p. 11.

principles which we may or may not obey, depending on whether we are "virtuous."

Kierkegaard brilliantly and boldly satirized his fellow Christians as geese who waddle to church to hear the gander, the pastor, honk and gabble about ethics and ideals and metaphysics; then they waddle back home, quacking about trivia all the while, and finally sit down to Sunday dinner—which is, of course, roast goose!! These same congregations of Christendom moved Nietzsche to declare that "God is dead," by which he meant, not that he killed him, but that he was simply remarking a cultural fact. Having observed the coming and going of German burghers and pastors and bureaucrats, he could only conclude with prophetic passion, "What are these churches now if they are not the tombs and sepulchers of God?" And Nietzsche's Zarathustra declaims, "Could it be possible! This old saint in the forest hath not yet heard of it, that God is dead!"[13] After Zarathustra is told by an old pope that he spent his whole life till the last hour serving that God, Zarathustra tells him: "For that old God liveth no more: he is indeed dead."[14]

What is Existentialism?
The Will Within or Without the Web?

It is commonplace that existentialism is too protean and various in its manifestations to permit an overall definition that will satisfy all observers and include all its practitioners; indeed, a suspicion of all "definitive" language is one of the characteristics of the movement. Nonetheless, certain qualities and orientations of thought and action emerge as one reads and reflects on existential philosophy, drama, novels, and poetry over the past century.

---

[13]Friedrich Nietzsche, *Thus Spake Zarathustra*, trans. by Thomas Common (New York: The Heritage Press, 1967), p. 5.
[14]*Ibid.*, p. 251.

Central to existential life and thought is that man discovers, sooner or later in his life, that he is an accident, that he merely "happens" or "has happened." He has been thrown or thrust into universe which did not ask his permission; and up until he consciously reflects on his "thrown-ness" (*Geworfenheit*-Heidegger), whether this occurs at age eighteen or forty-eight, he discovers also that he has been shaped by earthly powers (themselves also thrown into life) over which he had no control. This web of circumstance must be punctured; it must be penetrated. In a world in which he has been objectified, man must will himself, now that he has become self-conscious. He must not accept his condition, for that would be to live in "bad faith" (*mauvaise foi*). He must not perfunctorily agree that his will is reduced to merely performing actions which reveal a "nature" he has, for he has no nature; he has no essence. Acts which merely illustrate one's nature are superfluous; if one already possesses a nature, one need not achieve it by acting. His will is caught within the web of his history and experience, but one need not—indeed one *must* not—yield to that captivity. Just as the newborn infant screams in protest when he or she is pulled from the womb, held upside down in this strange topsy-turvy world, and then spanked crisply by the stinging hand of the physician, so he or she must constantly, in freedom, responsibility, and therefore, anxiety and anguish live without, or outside, this environmental web. Not to do this is to be absorbed into the environment into the same condition which the infant enjoyed in the womb. Man must will his existence, rather than live unconsciously in a womb of givens—nourishment, warmth, shelter, security. The will must constantly project (throw forth) the person into his future. This freedom constitutes our true human condition; it is not a nature or an essence; it is our "situation." We always live *in situ*. Given this condition, existentialism shares, it shares to me, the following categories of understanding: participation, personalism, presentism, and possibility.

Participation. Although existentialists have written and reflected as much as any other philosophers, they do so primarily to celebrate action, involvement, and passionate participation above reflection; thought is not superior to or a substitute for actual existence. When we think about things in the usual manner, we objectify them, and this turns being into having, presence into datum, persons into objects, and values into idols. Existentialists are fond of dramatic images and metaphors of acting and willing; for example, Kierkegaard's image of the man of faith living as if he were floating alone in 70,000 fathoms of water; Nietzsche's picture of man as a rope stretched over an abyss—between man and *Uebermensch*; or Pascal's portrayal of man already "embarked" on the voyage which he cannot avoid—therefore he must wager, he must risk, his life with a commitment.

Personalism. Subjectivity is prior for existentialism—not being *qua* being, but *my* being. When I choose to become who I am (the choosing one who wills), when I become self-conscious, I find myself estranged from the world of things. Sartre says the *pour-soi* (consciousness) differentiates itself from the *en-soi* (the objective world that is there). I must never give up my existence (*ex+sistere* = to stand outside of), my separateness, my uniqueness, to the world of *Da-Sein* (being-there), to the world of things, the *donnée*. To do so would be to lose consciousness, to become less than personal, and to become one of the tools or objects of experience, to live without authenticity and responsibility. Thus I must never give up my liberty to distinguish myself from other objects, including other selves.

Critics debate whether this radical jargon egoism leads to total epistemological subjectivism and/or ethical relativism or chaos. Sartre has agreed that, given the human condition, it matters not whether one gets drunk or becomes a leader of nations;[15] Camus has argued that since my free individual existence is always situated amongst other free persons, *mesure* or limitation is required, for no one can be totally free, if Sisyphus is to be happy as he rolls his stone up and down the mountain

---

[15]Jean-Paul Sartre, *Being and Nothingness*, trans. by Hazel E. Barnes (New York: Simon & Schuster, 1966), p. 797.

day after day.[16] Kierkegaard, as we have pointed out above, has stated dramatically that usual or conventional moral obligations, such as fatherly love for one's son, must paradoxically be suspended when God, himself the source of such paternal love, requires from the knight of faith a radical obedience. This extreme responsibility to choose gives birth to anguish and alienation. A. E. Housman writes:

> The laws of God, the laws of man,
> He may keep that will and can;
> Not I: let God and man decree
>
> Laws for themselves and not for me;
> And if my ways are not as theirs
> Let them mind their own affairs.
> Their deed I judge and much condemn,
> Yet when did I make laws for them?
> . . . .
> I a stranger and afraid
> In a world I never made.[17]

Presentism. Existentialists recognize the primacy of the present, for what am I other than what I am *no longer* (the past) and what I am *not yet* (the future)? Sartre is especially insistent that there is nothing in history or tradition to which we can appeal when we choose to act — no God whose acts we might remember, no code whose duties we must follow, and no examples whose pattern we might embody, ourselves. We are doomed to be free, moment by moment. There is no "divinity that shapes our ends, rough-hew them how we will"; nor is there a "special providence in the fall of a sparrow," as Hamlet declares in Act II/Scene 2. To rely on providence toward the past by which we are informed that God has revealed to us or

---

[16]Albert Camus, *L'Homme révolté* (Paris: Gallimard, 1951), p. 351.

[17]A. E. Housman, *Complete Poems* (New York: Holt, Rinehart and Winston, 1959), p. 111.

acted for us, so that we might hope in the promise of the future, is failure of nerve.

Camus has stated, "The future is the only world of transcendence for men without God."[18] We are not preserving anything when we act; we cannot follow Jesus Christ, when he says, "If you know these things, blessed are you if you do them" (John 13:17). We are merely and sheerly pro-jecting ourselves or hurling ourselves into the future. Having been thrown into the universe and caught in the web of circumstance without having been consulted or asked, we must throw ourselves forth (*pro +jacio*) toward the future, not to obey and enduring value system, not to reveal our character or essence, but to create ourselves through desire. Nietzsche called this the "transvaluation of values" by which the Overman (*Uebermensch*) would rise above the common herd morality into the aristocracy of the "joyful wisdom" that comes when one admits that the world has been washed clean of God's presence. One becomes strong enough to say "yes" to the cosmos which is a universe of bleak emptiness when it is not saturated with undeserved and indescribable pain. The "will to power" enables man to love this fate (*amor fati*), even though Nietzsche also taught the doctrine of the Eternal Return, by which he meant that " 'Twas ever thus"; things emerge and withdraw; events come and go; eras and powers cyclically rise and decline; yet a sureness remains. And that certainly is only that the present abides; there is no providence or eschatology. Yet one can and must choose or will one's self in the midst of this enthralling web.

Possibility. Nevertheless, Camus ended his great essay, "The Myth of Sisyphus," with the only good news he could proclaim—"One must imagine Sisyphus happy"; and we must remember that the essay begins with his famous dictum that the real burden of philosophy, the primary philosophical problem is that of suicide. In addition, Sartre stated at the beginning of "Existentialism,"

---

[18]L'Homme révolté, p. 207.

In any case, what can be said from the very beginning is that by existentialism we mean a doctrine which *makes human life possible* and, in addition, declares that every truth and every action implies a human setting and a human subjectivity.[19] (Italics mine)

By radical human freedom, subjective human beings may at present participate in the world, although without providence, and turn the web of experience from a prisonhouse into a world of possibility. On the one hand you have disillusioning monotony:

> Yonder see the morning blink:
>   The sun is up, and up must I,
> To wash and dress and eat and drink
> And look at things and talk and think
>   And work, and God knows why.
>
> Oh often have I washed and dressed
>   And what's to show for all my pain?
> Let me lie abed and rest:
> Ten thousand times I've done my best
>   And all's to do again.[20]

On the other hand, choice and projection and will become possible when I accept what is not merely *possible*, but what is absolutely real and inevitable—my death, what Camus called "the cruel mathematics of the universe": each *one* of us dies. Heidegger argues that once one admits that he is not only a being thrown into the world but also one who is thrown toward death (I came from nothing and I proceed toward nothing), he is enabled to overcome mere *Sorge* (care) and stark finitude (*Befindlichkeit*) and to live authentically within the bounds set for him. He is able to transcend his finite self and to choose his manner of participation. And it is noteworthy that Rudolph Bultmann, the existential Christian New Testament theologian

---

[19]"Existentialism," p. 447.
[20]*Complete Poems*, p. 110.

has used Heideggerian categories, as has Schubert Ogden, to re-cast his demythologized gospel into a reductionism that deprives all Christian revelation of content, in the name of self-authenticating decisionism.

Values in a Vacuum? All of this radical and challenging thought is undertaken in good faith to help us escape the vari-ous powers of modernity which oppress and disable modern humanity. First, there is the state, or statism, which produces Auden's anonymous cipher, "The Unknown Citizen":

> He was found by the Bureau of Statistics to be
> One against whom there was no official complaint,
> And all the reports on his conduct agree
> That, in the modern sense of an old-fashioned word, he was a
> saint,
> . . . .
> The Press are convinced that he bought a paper every day
> And that his reactions to advertisements were normal in
> every way.
> . . . .
> Our researchers into Public Opinion are content
> That he held the proper opinions for the time of year;
> When there was peace, he was for peace; when there was war, he
> went.
> . . . .
> Was he free? Was he happy? The question is absurd:
> Had anything been wrong, we should certainly have heard.[21]

Existentialists want man to hear and to be heard.

Second, there is the unhealthy dependence on scientism, the illegitimate son of a worthy father, science. Sigmund Freud pontificated: "No, science is no illusion. But it would be an illusion to suppose that we could get anywhere else what it cannot give us."[22] Robert Frost wittily calls scientism to task:

---

[21]W. H. Auden, p. 21.

[22]Sigmund Freud, *The Future of an Illusion* (New York: Liveright Publishing Corp., 1949), p. 98.

Sarcastic Science, she would like to know,
In her complacent ministry of fear,
How we propose to get away from here
When she has made things so we have to go
Or be wiped out. Will she be asked to show
Us how by rocket we may hope to steer
To some star off there, say, a half light-year
Through temperature of absolute zero?
Why wait for Science to supply the how
When any amateur can tell it now?
The way to get away should be the same
As fifty million years ago we came—
If any one remembers how that was.
I have a theory, but it hardly does.[23]

Whether or not existentialism "hardly does" will be discussed in the last section.

Third, mass production and economic fervor have caused us to fall into subhuman existence. As Gregor Samsa, the anti-hero of Kafka's *Metamorphosis*

. . . awoke one morning from a troubled dream, he found him-self changed in his bed to some monstrous kind of vermin.

He lay on his back, which was as hard as armor plate, and raising his head a little, he could see the arch of his great brown belly, divided by bowed corrugations. The bedcover was slipping helplessly off the summit of the curve, and Gregor's legs, pitiably thin compared with their former size, fluttered helplessly before his eyes.

"What has happened?", he thought. It was no dream.[24]

This revolting and repulsive metaphor is not to be taken as fantastic and incredible, for Gregor has actually been living as an insect:

---

[23]Edward Connery Lathem, ed., *The Poetry of Robert Frost* (New York: Holt, Rinehart and Winston, 1969), p. 395.

[24]Franz Kafka, *The Metamorphosis* in *Short Novels of the Masters*, ed. Charles Neider (NY: Holt, Rinehart & Winston, Inc., 1961), p. 537.

"God!", he thought, "What a job I've chosen. Traveling day in, day out. A much more worrying occupation than working in the office! And apart from business itself, this plague of traveling: the anxieties of exchanging trains, the irregular, inferior meals, the ever-changing faces, never to be seen again, people with whom one has no chance to be friendly. To hell with it all!"[25]

Note that the passage ironically begins with "God," and ends with "hell."

Fourth, rationalism has seduced man into confidently thinking that he can comprehend life, either through enlightenment empiricism, or Hegelian panlogism. In "The Death of Ivan Ilych," we find Ivan slowly and painfully dying from cancer in the midst of his social and vocational success; and he remembers, lying abed with emotional terror and physical agony, how he had been taught the syllogism as a youth in school:

The syllogism he had learnt from Kiezewetter's Logic: "Caius is a man, men are mortal, therefore Caius is mortal," had always seemed to him correct as applied to Caius, but certainly not as applied to himself. That Caius — man in the abstract — was mortal, was perfectly correct, but he was not Caius, not an abstract man, but a creature quite, quite separate from all others. He had been little Vanya, with a mamma and a papa, with Mitya and Volodya, with the toys, a coachman and a nurse, afterwards with Katenka and with all the joys, griefs and delights of childhood, boyhood, and youth. What did Caius know of the smell of that striped leather ball Vanya had been so fond of? Had Caius kissed his mother's hand like that, and did the silk of her dress rustle so for Caius? Had he rioted like that at school when the pastry was bad? Had Caius been in love with that? Could Caius preside at a session as he did? Caius really was mortal, and it was right for him to die; but for me, little Vanya, Ivan Ilych, with all my thoughts and emotions, it's altogether a different

---

[25]*Ibid.*, pp. 537–538.

matter. It cannot be that I ought to die. That would be too terrible.[26]

Man has lost his passion, his freedom, his involvement because rationalism has wrongly claimed him by deluding him into detachment, rather than helping him to accurately and personally understand the world.

Finally, metaphysics has falsely intrigued us into imagining that there is a world above, or below, or outside this one, from whence we come (the doctrine of creation), by which we are preserved (the doctrine of providence), which has been penetrated for our salvation (the doctrine of salvation), and toward which we are called (eschatology). Stephen Crane frankly dramatizes this situation:

A MAN SAID TO THE UNIVERSE

A man said to the universe:
"Sir, I exist!"
"However," replied the universe,
"The fact has not created in me
A sense of obligation."[27]

Existence is a mere fact; our facticity engulfs us into a cosmos that is inert and dead; it is indifferent.

Meursault, the main character of Camus's *The Stranger*, calls it a "benign indifference";[28] but it is debatable that a world whose origin and fulcrum is indifference can muster a world of values by which we can live. Radical existential response to such a world is the only way we can live authentically; we must not permit the "facts" to "factualize" us. The web of the world either captures man's will so that he chooses to make love, to

---

[26]Leo Tolstoy, "The Death of Ivan Ilych," in *Eleven Modern Short Novels*, p. 34.

[27]Stephen Crane, "A Man Said to the Universe," in *The Modern Age*, ed. by Leonard Lief and James F. Light (New York: Holt, Rinehart, and Winston, 1976), p. 160.

[28]Albert Camus, *The Stranger*, trans. by Stuart Gilbert (New York: Random House, 1946), p. 154.

cook a spaghetti dinner, to take a swim, or to go to the office indifferently—which is the manner in which Meursault lives. To Marie's concern about whether he loves her, "I said that sort of question had no meaning, really; but I supposed I didn't."[29] On the other hand, such a universe captivates him, seducing him into thinking that anarchy is freedom, that sheer subjectivity is actually liberty, and that man is free to create himself and his values. However, one is not free when one is able to do as one pleases or wishes; one is truly free when one is free to do what one ought to do. What ought one to do?

A Christian Response:
Revelation and Reason in Retrospect and Prospect

Revelation and Reason. I have thus far tried to expound in brief and in general the "nature" (!) of existentialism, with only occasional critical evaluation. In this last section, I shall endeavor to respond to the challenge.

First of all, it needs to be said that existentialism has rightly called into question the hubristic hyperconfidence in man's autonomous reason that the Enlightenment produced. Although one usually thinks of Hegel's attempt to comprehend universal mind with his own, it is also true that Baconian empiricism and Kantian moral reason also needed critique. Insofar as it delimits reason and points out its conditioned perspective, existentialism—at least theistic existentialism—rightly opens the world to God's sovereign revelational gift of Himself. The point is not that God ignores reason and that the Judeo-Christian faith is irrational, for that would give up the world of philosophical, ethical, and scientific discourse to the secularists whose methodological myopia constantly rules out the possibility that God created or acts in the world. For example, many scientists insist *a priori* that Jesus could not have been raised

---

[29]*Ibid.*, p. 44.

from the dead since we have no modern or historical analogies for this. However, Wolfhart Pannenberg has argued:

> The possibility of the historicity of Jesus' resurrection has been opposed on the grounds that the resurrection of a dead person even in the sense of the resurrection to imperishable life would be an event that violates the laws of nature. Yet . . . only a part of the laws of nature are ever known. Further, in a world that as a whole represents a singular, irreversible process, an individual event is never completely determined by natural laws. Conformity to law embraces only one aspect of what happens. From another perspective, every thing that happens is contingent. . . . The judgment about whether an event, however unfamiliar, has happened or not is in the final analysis a matter for the historian and cannot be prejudged by the knowledge of natural science.[30]

Thus, reason is essential to religious discourse and behavior. However, since all humanity, including rationalists and existentialists, are caught in the web of being and are blinded by it because of willfully ignoring or misunderstanding the nature of things (Romans 1:18–23), God must reveal Himself, for all of man is flawed by the fall—his passion, his imagination, his reason. This being the case, it should not surprise us that Roquentin, the anti-hero of Sartre's novel, *Nausea*, is repulsed by the very thingness of things—pebbles, bedsheets, books, legs, glasses—for he has no means by which his own consciousness (*pour-soi*) might see that the world of things (*en-soi*) is nonetheless God's world. Roquentin reflects:

> The *true* sea is cold and black, full of animals; it crawls under this thin green film made to deceive human beings. The sylphs all round me have let themselves be taken in: they only see the thin film, which proves the existence of God. I see beneath it! . . . Things are divorced from their names. They are there, grotesque, headstrong, gigantic, and it seems ridiculous to call them seats or say anything at all about them: I am in the midst of

---

[30]Wolfart Pannenberg, *Jesus, God and Man*, trans. by Lewis L. Wilkins and Duane A. Priebe (Philadelphia: The Westminster Press, 1968), p. 98.

things, nameless things. Alone, without words, defenseless, they surround me, are beneath me, behind me, above me. They demand nothing, they don't impose themselves: they are there.[31]

Gerard Manley Hopkins, however, did not see the world as gross or grotesque, but as the scene of God's glory:

NOTHING is so beautiful as Spring—
 When weeds, in wheels, shoot long and lovely and lush;
 Thrush's eggs look little low heavens, and thrush
Through the echoing timber does so rinse and wring
The ear, it strikes like lightnings to hear him sing;
 The glassy peartree leaves and blooms, they brush
 The descending blue; that blue is all in a rush
With richness; the racing lambs too have fair their fling.

What is all this juice and all this joy?
 A strain of the earth's sweet being in the beginning
In Eden garden.—Have, get, before it cloy,

 Before it cloud, Christ, lord, and sour with shining,
Innocent mind and Mayday in girl and boy,
 Most, O maid's child, thy choice and worthy the winning.[32]
. . . .
And for all this, nature is never spent;
 There lives the dearest freshness deep down things;
And though the last lights off the black West went
 Oh, morning, at the brown brink eastward, springs—
Because the Holy Ghost over the bent
 World broods with warm breast and with ah! bright
 wings.[33]

This perspective of Hopkins' is a response to God's gift of revelation. Notice two things: it is a "shaped faith" that he expresses through the poetic structure, and it is a personal faith

---

[31]Jean-Paul Sartre, *Nausea*, trans. by Lloyd Alexander (New York: New Directions, 1964), pp. 167-68, 169.

[32]W. H. Gardner and N. H. MacKenzie, eds., *The Poems of Gerald Manley Hopkins* (London: Oxford University Press, 1967), p. 67.

[33]*Hopkins*, p. 66.

and trust *by which* the Christian believes *the* faith, the deposit of truth, *about* God. Existentialists minimize the role of reason in the name of passion and freedom and subjectivity, but they do so at grave risk, for man is made in the image of God (Genesis 1:26) and this means that man's self-consciousness includes our complete conative reflection and behavior—reason, will, affections. Man's consciousness is not mere *self-*consciousness; it is genuinely self-conscious when it becomes aware that we are creatures of God.

Befindlichkeit (finitude) is not a sin or a burden. It is openness to Being-Itself, or God, and must include the exercise of the reason to prevent us from falling into the abyss of sheer freedom, stark cosmology, and indifferent ethics. Jacques Ellul has said:

> Reason does not represent a "trick" but is really the result of an effort to find something that is neither an external constraint nor interiorized social imperatives and that will allow a man to be free and yet at the same time choose a behavior and express opinions which are communicable and can be recognized as acceptable and shared by the other members of the tribe. Here precisely we have the magnificent discovery made by the West: that the individual's whole life can be, and even is, the subtle, infinitely delicate interplay of reason and freedom.[34]

God reveals Himself in creation and redemption in which the *logos* who was from the beginning manifests himself in Jesus Christ (John 1:1, 1:14) and also enlightens everyone who comes into the world (John 1:9). Pascal, one of the greatest existentialists, wrote:

> Man is obviously made to think. It is his whole dignity and his whole merit; and his whole duty is to think as he ought. Now, the order of thought is to begin with self, and with its Author and its end. . . . If we submit everything to reason, our religion

---

[34]Jacques Ellul, *The Betrayal of the West*, trans. by Matthew J. O'Connell (New York: The Seabury Press, 1978), pp. 44–45.

will have no mysterious and supernatural element. If we offend the principles of reason, our religion will be absurd and ridiculous.[35]

Only then, does Pascal offer his most quoted aphorism: "The heart has its reasons, which reason does not know."[36]

Thus, humanity is not gratuitously thrown into the world; we are not mere projects, existing without an essence; we are created in the image of God, and the *logos* enlightens us all. It is this cardinal truth that makes the existential quest possible, for any attempt to understand the meaning and purpose of God is the reflection, however bedimmed, of God's eternal light. If the existentialists are right, then there can be no intelligible revelation of the God of creation, love, truth, righteousness, and redemption, for there is only atomistic existence. If God is only sheer will, then there is no nature (although there is mankind), so how could there be grace or value? In short, how is the human enterprise at all valid, if essence does not exist? Jacques Maritain has rightly declared:

> An existence without an essence, a subject without essence; from the very beginning we dwell in the unthinkable. . . . For if you abolish essence, or that which *esse* posits, by that very act you abolish existence, or *esse*. Those two notions are correlative and inseparable. An existentialism of this sort is self-destroying.[37]

A true existentialism is an ". . . existential realism, the confrontation of the act of existing by an intelligence determined never to disown itself."[38] This does not deny the depth and mystery and personal uniqueness or freedom of each person, nor the transcendence and mystery of God, for

---

[35]Blaise Pascal, *Pensées*, trans. by W. F. Trotter, in *Great Books of the Western World*, Vol. 23 (Chicago: Encyclopaedia Inc., 1952), pp. 200, 222.

[36]*Pensées*, p. 222.

[37]Jacques Maritain, *Existence and the Existent* (Garden City: Image Books, 1961), pp. 13, 15.

[38]*Ibid.*, p. 12.

. . . only subjects exist, with the accidents which inhere in them, the action which emanates from them, and the relations which they bear to one another. Only individual subjects exercise the act of existing.

What we call *subject* St. Thomas called *suppositum*. Essence is *that which* a thing is; suppositum is *that which* has an essence, *that which* exercises existence and action — *actiones sunt suppositorum — that which* subsists.[39]

Therefore,

The subject, or suppositum, or person has an essence, an essential structure. . . . It is a very simple-minded error to believe that subjectivity possesses no intelligible structure, on the ground that it is an inexhaustible depth; and to conceive of it as without any nature whatsoever for the purpose of making it an absurd abyss of pure and formless liberty.[40]

In revelation, God comes to us personally; hence, existential passion and suffering; and he also gives us his truth, moral law as an objective standard, which is knowable, requires obedience, and is a joy to follow. Man does not project himself, or make himself; he is created by God and reflects the *logos* by his own reflection on and doing of "these things."

Finally, brethren, whatever is true, whatever is honorable, whatever is just, whatever is pure, whatever is lovely, whatever is gracious, if there is any excellence, if there is anything worthy of praise, *think* about these things. What you have learned and received and heard and seen in me, *do*; and the God of peace will be with you. (Philippians 4:8-9) (Italics mine)

The Bible combines thinking and doing; in fact, the Bible is the inspired revelation of God's nature and the inspired record of his acts, and all of this has to do with ethics, or values. The decalogue, the sermon on the mount, the great command-

---

[39]*Ibid.*, p. 70.
[40]*Ibid.*, pp. 87-88.

ment—these all give objective content to answer the question, "What ought I to do?" Sartre arbitrarily claims:

> . . . there can no longer be an *a priori* Good, since there is no infinite and perfect consciousness to think it. Nowhere is it written that the Good exists, that we must be honest, that we must not lie; because the fact is we are on a plane where there are only men.[41]

It is precisely on this "plane where there are only men" that God has secured ethical laws based on his transcendent love, righteousness, and will.

Retrospect and Prospect. In retrospect, then, we turn to our tradition, back through the councils and the creeds (themselves sources of wisdom) to the Bible; and this is not *mauvaise foi* or failure of nerve. We know our condition and nature before God and our fellow men through the witness of the prophets and apostles who themselves acknowledged Messiah. For example, biblical witness rightly depicts the value of human beings when it records Jesus' statement, "Fear not, therefore; you are of more value than many sparrows" (Matt. 10:31). It is in claims such as these that humanity finds its source and hope. Since we are each created in God's image, the neighbor becomes my opportunity for genuine human fellowship. Instead of seeing the neighbor's gaze as a threat by which he fixes me and objectifies me, I see him in his creaturehood and possibility under God, and thus I am moved to love God, neighbor, and self, which the Great Commandment, on which hangs all the law and the prophets, requires me to do (Matt. 22:34–40). In Gabriel Marcel's terms, I am *disponible*; I am available to my neighbor because God is available to all. Contrary to Sartre's assertion, "Even if God did exist, that would change nothing," the response to the existentialist challenge must be that we cannot permit objective Christian moral values to evaporate into naked freedom. It is true that Sartre speaks of inter-subjectivity—being-for-others (*pour-autrui*); but surely this is a

---

[41]"Existentialism," p. 451.

non sequitur. Such claims are ineffective, for they are ground-
less; they have no transcendent source.

And yet . . . and yet, the gift of revelation, the responsibility
to exercise reason, and the retrospective look to the past can
themselves turn us into pillars of salt rather than into the salt of
the earth with *prospects* for the future, unless we heed the
challenge of earnest existentialists. When the existentialist sees
human beings ignore the actual human condition; when he sees
blue-collar and white-collar convention palmed off as divine
command, he wishes to shake us loose from comfortable morality, for "The absolute duty may cause one to do what ethics
would forbid, but by no means can it cause the knight of faith
to cease to love."[42] Such a rarified ethical situation is rarely
heard in suburbs where a green lawn and white yacht must be
maintained, or on a college campus where jobbism trains men
and women for employment slots; thus we produce skilled *vir-
tuosi* who rarely question the virtues and values they have been
taught. The Jews were liberated through the love of God in
Egypt and the law of God at Sinai; the Greeks were liberated
when, although they did not know Jahweh or Jesus, they saw
that human reason, through dividing and defining, produces
the "philosophic habit" of the liberated man; and the Romans
introduced civic law and thus civil liberties, although never perfectly. Perhaps the existential challenge to Christian values is to
provoke us to claim our tradition more authentically and more
relevantly, without hypocrisy or *hubris*, and with greater passion and power.

The title of this essay mentions "Sheer Freedom," "Shaped
Faith," and "Terminal Terminology." Sheer freedom (without a
transcendent source, the tradition, or a nature) is no alternative
to shaped faith (formed by the biblical structure, grounded in
the truthful revelation of the eternal God, defined and controlled by the reason, and motivated by the enthusiasm of the
passions). Existential freedom is transient and chaotic, for its
sheerness is transparent; once it is subject to scrutiny, it reveals

---

[42]*Fear and Trembling*, p. 84.

that there is a cipher, a void, at its center. Thus, such a sheer freedom demonstrates that not only does the emperor have no clothes, there is no emperor to wear them. Further, atheistic existentialism sheers or diverts us away from our foundations in the Judeo-Christian tradition and our transcendent God who has created us in his image. The question from *Hamlet*, "Who's there?" should be answered, "God is!" And he has not left himself without a witness, for there is a "Truth which is not from man";[43] this truth has, nevertheless, spoken to man *through* man, and that veracity is invaluable.

---

[43]Emil Brunner, *Our Faith*, trans. by John W. Rilling (New York: Scribner's Sons, 1936), Foreword.

Meaning and Morality: Analytic Ethics in the Twentieth Century

Keith Yandell

Dr. Keith E. Yandell received his B. A. in history and philosophy (1959) and M. A. in philosophy (1960) at Wayne State University. He received his Ph. D. in philosophy at Ohio State University (1966). He has taught philosophy at several colleges and universities, including Kings College, Ohio State, and, since 1966, at the University of Wisconsin in Madison where he is a professor of South Asian Studies and currently chairman of the department of philosophy. He has published seven books on ethics, Christianity, and philosophy, including *Basic Issues in the Philosophy of Religion* (1971); *Ockham, Descartes, and Hume* with William Courtenay and William H. Hay (1977); and *Christianity and Contemporary Philosophy* (1983). He has authored over forty articles and book reviews in numerous religion and scholarly journals. Dr. Yandell has also received several fellowships from the University of Wisconsin and the National Endowment for the Humanities.

Introduction

In Plato and Aristotle, Augustine and Aquinas, Kant and Mill, and even Hutcheson and Hume, there was agreement on what it seems fair to call "ethical rationalism": the view that a moral principle, rule, or judgment is either true, or else false, and that we often are able, in particular cases, to determine which.

To a considerable extent, the early history of Anglo-American ethics in this century can be plausibly seen as a retreat from ethical rationalism. Since, if no moral claim is either true or false—if there really *are* no moral claims—or if one cannot tell which moral claims, if any, are true, then there really is no such discipline as ethics, and the early history of Anglo-American ethics in this century can be plausibly seen as a retreat from ethics itself.

Ethical *intuitionism*, represented here by G. E. Moore and W. D. Ross, was a variety of ethical rationalism, but one of the slenderest varieties. Thus the shift to *emotivism*, as propounded by A. J. Ayer and Charles Stevenson, represented less of a contrast than might be expected when reason gives way to feeling. The rather flagrant inadequacies of emotivism, whether in Ayer's simple or Stevenson's sophisticated version, led to its revision in terms of R. M. Hare's *prescriptivism*. The inadequacies of prescriptivism, in turn, led to a slow but steady reinstatement of traditional moral philosophy.

There are works, and figures, that play an important role in the moral philosophy of contemporary Anglo-America which cannot be more than mentioned, but deserve at least a passing reference. Stephen Toulmin's *The Place of Reason in Ethics* at least admitted that reason had a place there. Marcus Singer's *Generalization in Ethics* restored moral philosophy to a central place in philosophical reflection; it even located ethics in the humanities (and, at that, not as part of the philosophy of language). Henry Veatch's *Rational Man* and *Toward an Ontology of Morals* defended a type of natural-law tradition. William Frankena's *Ethics* defended unrepentant ethical rationalism. Here, and elsewhere, ethics survived, and even to an extent flourished, while nonetheless the loudest (though not therefore the deepest) voices questioned the very possibility of moral knowledge.

When one, nowadays, turns the pages of Alan Donagan's *The Theory of Morality* or Mary Midgley's *Beast and Man*, *Heart and Mind*, or *Wickedness: A Philosophical Essay*, one finds again discussions of human nature, fundamental types of ethical systems, and substantive moral issues. Moral skepticism is not dead, nor is it likely to die. But non-skeptics are not looked at as upholders of impossible views, and serious moral reflection about ecological, medical, and social issues is a recognized need. Moral philosophy of a sort plainly continuous with traditional ethics has returned.

My task here is to trace, albeit briefly, the outlines of this history of moral philosophy from anemia to comatose state to vibrant health in twentieth-century Anglo-American thought. My approach will be conceptual in that I will trace theses and arguments rather than dates and events. But there has been a genuine dialectic on these issues in contemporary analytic philosophy, and I think that in this case history is not falsified by its being organized conceptually.

Intuitionism

Ethical intuitionism is a variety, though one of the slenderest varieties, of ethical rationalism. Its proponents were potent critics. In such works as E. F. Carritt, *The Theory of Morals*, G. E. Moore, *Ethics*, A. C. Ewing, *Ethics*, and W. D. Ross, *The Right and the Good* and the *Foundations of Ethics*, one finds powerful criticisms of such views as subjectivism, hedonism, and utilitarianism. I think it is fair to say that they refuted such views as "what is right is just what I (or what my society) approve of," "only pleasure is rightly valued for its own sake," and "what is actually right varies from culture to culture," and they called into serious question the thesis that the right action for an agent on a given occasion is that action which, of those available to the agent, will maximize goodness. Critique was their greatest strength, and they were formidable in its exercise.

Still, when it came to offering a positive ethical theory, the intuitionists were less formidable. Endeavoring to build on the fact that—as Bertrand Russell once put it—an argument must begin somewhere, the intuitionists insisted on attempting to begin with something self-evident or indubitable. Moral reasoning, they held, must begin with either one or more moral principles which are allegedly evident to reason or with particular moral judgments (e.g., "It would be wrong to deceive Mary about my having lost the cat") which also were alleged to be self-evident.

The means of knowledge of such self-evident or indubitable propositions — be they principles or particular moral claims — was simply *seeing them to be true*, rather in the manner that one either sees (or else fails to see) that nothing can have incompatible properties, or that if A is a *simple* thing (not a class or complex) and A ceases to exist at time t1, then nothing that exists at t3 can be numerically identical with A, no matter how similar to A it may be.

Of course, one can defend non-inferred, basic claims in various ways. One can argue dialectically for them, asking one who doubts them to consider what else one must abandon if one abandons them. For example, if it is claimed that a proposition can be true and false at the same time and in the same respect, one can reply, "Yes, you are right; nothing can be true and false in the same respect at the same time" and upon being informed that this denies what was asserted, can reply again that on the asserter's own view this is compatible with its also asserting the same thing the asserter said. Or one can note the fundamental role that the basic proposition plays in a conceptual system which itself is in some manner highly confirmed. Or one can for the moment elevate one set of basic propositions above suspicion and test others in their light, and by shifting the membership of the elevated set come in the long run to testing each basic proposition without supposing any to be self-evident. But one feature of Moore's views perhaps served to keep these, and other, possibilities of testing non-derived moral propositions in the background if not altogether out of sight.

Moore distinguished between *the good*, which he held to be a complex, and what *good* refers to, which he held to be a simple, unanalyzable, non-natural property. For something to be good was simply for it to have that property. Further, whether or not something has that property was to be discovered, as it were, introspectively. In *A Short History of Ethics*, Alasdair MacIntyre writes:

Moore takes it that the things which ought to exist for their own sake are those which we call intrinsically good. How do we know what is intrinsically good? The answer is that we cannot fail to recognize the property of intrinsic goodness when confronted with it. Propositions concerning what is intrinsically good—as contrasted with what is good only because it is a means to something intrinsically good—are susceptible neither of proof nor of disproof. This is because *good* is the name of a simple, unanalyzable property . . .[1]

Moore himself wrote in his *magnum opus, Principia Ethica,* to this effect:

I have tried in this book to distinguish clearly two kinds of questions . . . What kind of things ought to exist for their own sakes? . . . What kind of actions ought we to perform? . . . Once we recognize the exact meaning of the two questions, I think it also becomes plain what kind of reasons are relevant as arguments for or against any particular answer to them. It becomes plain that, for answers to the *first* question, no relevant experience whatever can be adduced: from no other truth, except themselves alone, can it be inferred that they are either true or false. We can guard against error only by taking care, that, when we try to answer a question of this kind, we have before our minds that question only, and not some other or others . . .[2]

When we try to answer the question, "Is X (intrinsically) good?", then, we are—according to Moore—asking whether X ought to exist for its own sake. More to the present point, we are asking whether X has a certain unanalyzable non-natural property *goodness*, the presence of which is to be introspectively or observationally discerned, nor inferred.

It is only fair to note here that Moore has his reservations about intuitionism. In *Principia*, he writes that

---

[1] Alasdair MacIntyre, *A Short History of Ethics* (New York: Macmillan, 1966), p. 249.

[2] G. E. Moore, *Principia Ethica* (London: Cambridge University Press, 1971), pp. vii–viii.

in order to express the fact that ethical propositions of my *first* class (those that purport to tell us what is intrinsically good) are incapable of proof or disproof, I have sometimes followed Sidgwick's usage in calling them "Intuitions." But it may be noticed that I am not an "Intuitionist" in the ordinary sense of the term. . . . The Intuitionist proper is distinguished by maintaining that propositions of my *second* class — propositions which assert that a certain action is *right* or a *duty* — are incapable of proof or disproof by any inquiry into the results of such actions. I, on the contrary, am no less anxious to maintain that propositions of *this* kind are *not* "Intuitions" than to maintain that propositions of my *first* class *are* Intuitions.[3]

But, for all that, Moore is — even on his own terms — an intuitionist regarding any answer to the question as to whether or not something is intrinsically good. Any such question, apparently, is to be decided by non-sensory observation of a non-natural property (if the item in question *is* intrinsically good) or by the non-sensory non-observation of a non-natural property — the failure to non-sensorily observe it (if the item in question lacks intrinsic goodness).

W. D. Ross adds worthy complications to Moore's perspective. Recognizing the complexity of moral reasoning, Ross adds the doctrine of duties that we have "on the whole" or "unless overridden by stronger duties." In cases of conflict of duties, one may have to reflect on which duty, under the prevailing circumstances, is more weighty. Here (as Moore too insisted) there is a role for moral reasoning that goes beyond intuiting alleged non-natural properties. More important, as Moore leaves things, it appears that the property *goodness* is not tightly connected with other properties. Ross views it as a "consequential" or "dependent" or "supervenient" property — a property that, say, a person has because he has deep integrity or an action has because it will alleviate great suffering. His insistence that goodness "supervenes" on, or is a function of, other

---

[3]*Ibid.*

properties seems correct. This is an important improvement over Moore.

Geoffrey Warnock, in *Contemporary Moral Philosophy*, writes that:

> For Moore, there is no reason why what is good is good — that it *is* good is not only a distinguishable, but a totally isolated, fact about it, not just different from, but unrelated to, anything else. But if so, then it seems that morality is not only not reducible to, or identifiable with, any ordinary features of the world or of human beings; it seems to stand in absolutely no relation to any such features, and to be, in the strictest sense, entirely inexplicable. The picture presented is that of a realm of moral qualities, *sui generis*, and indefinable, floating, as it were, quite free from anything else whatever, but cropping up here and there, quite contingently and for no reason, in bare conjunction with more ordinary features of the everyday world.[4]

Yet even with Ross the problem remains as to how we are to discern the moral facts of a case.

Various problems, of course, arise when one reflects on Moore's views. The notion of a "non-natural" property is hardly lucid, and Moore later admitted that he had never made it clear. While it is true, no doubt, that some propositions are such that one either sees them to be true or else lives without the benefits of such knowledge — the proposition that nothing can have incompatible properties is perhaps the most-cited example — it is not clear that even in these cases nothing can be said on behalf of the propositions in question other than that one either sees them or not. For example, one who does not know that the principle of non-contradiction is true may nonetheless see that he does not both know and not know this, nor could he, and thus may come to see that the reasons why this is not possible are such as to legitimize his braving the claim that no contradiction ever attains truth.

---

[4]Geoffrey Warnock, *Contemporary Moral Philosophy* (New York: St. Martin's Press, 1967), p. 14.

Or one might see that to the degree that the principle of non-contradiction is in doubt, to that degree it is also in doubt whether our knowing it to be false would be the slightest barrier to our also knowing it to be true. To put the point briefly, such propositions as are seen to be true are also, sometimes at least, dialectically defensible. One is not left simply trying harder to introspectively discover some non-natural characteristic, or (as Moore would agree) some self-certifying inner state.

Further, moral principles—the utility principle, or Kant's categorical imperative, for example—and principles that ascribe intrinsic goodness to some object or state are plainly the objects of much debate. Arguments are offered against them as well as on their behalf, and, at the least, if they are somehow self-evident to a clear and discerning intelligence, there are ways of sorting out bad objections and mistaken implications so that one's mind can approach clarity about relevant matters with the hope that discernment may dawn. A moral principle may be basic in that it follows from no other moral claim that is more clearly true, and that it follows also from no non-moral claim. But this does not mean that arguments against it may not be assessed, or that arguments—at least of a dialectical sort—may not be made on its behalf. One can still argue "and if you deny the truth of this principle, then . . . "; and if one can fill in the blank with falsehoods one must then embrace or truths one must then forego, one has argued impressively for the principle in question without having claimed to discover more obvious claims from which it follows. Thus, appeal to intuitions cannot be the whole, or even most, of the story in the epistemology of ethics, and discernment of non-natural properties plays little if any role in assessing moral claims.

Emotivism

Various factors promoted emotivism. One was that it is not obvious that moral claims satisfy a correspondent criterion for truth. A true statement corresponds to some existing state of affairs. But to what state of affairs does *Pointless killing is wrong* correspond? Another was the alleged fact of cultural relativism. What, morally speaking, will play in Polynesia will not play in Peoria; very diverse moral practices obtain in different parts of the world. This fact was widely taken to support moral relativism — sometimes on the ground that it showed there is no universal conscience or moral sense, sometimes on the ground that there is no rational basis for deciding which of conflicting moral views are correct. A third was the conceptual thinness of the intuitionism which preceded emotivism. If moral reason must speak through an intuitionist perspective, its voice will seem muted.

Of course, as we shall see, it is hardly lucid that the verification principle on which emotivism depends itself corresponds to any state of affairs; indeed, for reasons we will note, verificationism is plainly false.

Regarding cultural relativism, three things should be said. One is that it is not so clear as one might think that it is true, and, insofar as there is moral diversity from culture to culture, it is not clear that it is as widespread as is often believed. The point is worth underlining. Perhaps the simplest way to make it requires distinguishing between moral principles and moral rules. A moral rule specifies a particular class of actions which it commends as right or condemns as wrong, though it specifies no reason why this is so. A moral principle specifies one or more reasons why a class of actions is right (or wrong), though it offers no such judgment on any specific class of actions. Thus, *Torture for pleasure is wrong* states a moral rule; *It is always wrong to treat a person as a means only, and not also as an end* expresses a moral principle. *Basic* moral disagreement is disagreement regarding moral principles. Differences in morally relevant behavior, in fact, need not reflect differences concerning moral rules or moral principles; they may reflect sheer differences about what the descriptive situation is. A difference between the moral practices of two societies proves a moral difference only if it cannot be explained on the basis of the same moral principles being differently applied to a common view of the descriptive circumstances or being applied to differently described circumstances. But the very complex questions that applying these considerations to cross-cultural differences in moral practices would involve are hardly if ever raised. So it is simply not clear to what degree cultural relativism is true.

More important is the fact that the truth of moral relativism does not follow from the truth, however widely established, of cultural relativism. The fallacy of disparity (which compares scientific beliefs — a belief being scientific only if it passes rigorous tests, and moral beliefs — a belief being moral if it is about ethics and someone holds it, to the disadvantage of the latter) often occurs in discussions of moral and cultural relativity, and often obscures the otherwise clear fact that disagreement about a topic is possible only if someone can be right about it.

Emotivism was classically expressed in A. J. Ayer's early and outrageous book *Language, Truth, and Logic.* The core doctrine of this book was that *being meaningful* (in the sense of *being either true or else false*) is identical to *being true or false by definition* (being a tautology or a contradiction), or *being empirically confirmable or disconfirmable by direct observation* (observation alone, rather than observation plus inference), of *following from a class of statements every member of which meets one or the other of these criteria.* The inelegant though philosophically informative history of this movement has often been told, and one can follow it in A. J. Ayer, ed., *Logical Positivism,* or Alvin Plantinga's *God and Other Minds,* or the present author's *Basic Issues in the Philosophy of Religion.* Suffice it to say that this doctrine about what *being meaningful* amounted to — a doctrine classically called the *verification principle* or criterion of meaning — has the unfortunate problem of being meaningless on its own criterion. Attempts were made to dismiss this fact by saying such things as "Weighing machines are not expected to weigh themselves," but the inconvenient fact remained that a doctrine whose truth is incompatible with its own meaningfulness (and hence incompatible with its own truth) is an embarrassment to its propounders, and Ayer himself later confessed, "We were wrong." A curious, and no doubt very frustrating, further fact was (as can be seen from any of the accounts of its history mentioned above) that the actual attempts to formulate a version of the verification principle (and many versions were offered) on which nothing clearly meaningful was kept out and nothing clearly nonsensical was allowed in failed miserably, without exception. A theory about ethics with this sort of epistemological backing has little going for it.

Still, the theory was at least clear. What one "means" by saying "Torture for pleasure is wrong" is not "By an objective standard, torture for pleasure is to be morally condemned" or even "Torture for pleasure does not elicit my favor," but rather something that might be expressed by "Torture for pleasure, boo!" Analogously, "Honesty is right," on Ayer's theory, is properly rendered in some such terms as "Hurrah for honesty." Such locutions *express* feelings. They do not report our having them, for such reports are (in contrast to ethical sentences, on the theory in question) true or false. This, essentially, was Ayer's version of emotivism.

Besides its shaky epistemological underpinnings, which seem its only real answer to the question, "Why should anyone *accept* this theory?", it had other weaknesses. For one thing, moral claims do appear in arguments, and their presence seems appropriate. The argument *Spreading broken glass on the carpet will cause much pointless pain: causing pointless pain is wrong; so spreading broken glass on the carpet is wrong* seems quite in order — both sound and valid. But, since only meaningful statements can appear as premises in arguments, according to emotivism this argument is really not an argument at all but is identical to *Spreading broken glass on the carpet will cause much pointless pain; causing pointless pain: Boo! Spreading glass on the carpet: Boo!* There is high implausibility in the suggestion that this really is an adequate restatement of the argument — an implausibility that transfers properly to the theory that suggests this "restatement."

Further, given emotivism, if person A thinks that abortion on demand is right, and person B thinks that abortion on demand is wrong, they do not disagree; A is merely saying "Abortion on demand: yuk!", and B is merely saying "Abortion on demand: yea! They differ merely as two persons, one of whom loves chunky peanut butter but despises creamy while the other loves creamy peanut butter but despises chunky. This trivialization by evaporation of any and all moral disputes appears both silly and callous, and I know of no good reason to think that the appearances here are deceptive.

Charles Stevenson's more complex version of emotivism intended to overcome objections to Ayer's simpler version. Two words can share descriptive content but have diverse emotive meanings. Thus, "male person with developed muscle" may share its descriptive content with "musclebound monster" and "Greek god." Similarly, two moral terms may share descriptive content but reflect very different assessment or attitude. Stevenson does not deny that moral terms designate properties and have descriptive content, but this he holds not to be what makes them *moral* terms. Moral terms convey attitudes, and moral judgments have as their basic role the influencing of the persons to whom they are addressed. Thus, if you tell me, "It is good to pay one's debts," you are endeavoring to influence my attitude to debt-paying, to strengthen my already positive attitude toward this activity, or to create such an attitude in me if I lack it, or the like. What is distinctively *moral* about moral principles, rules, judgments or the like is their attitude-expressing and attitude-affecting capacity. As Stevenson put it in an essay entitled, "Ethical Judgments and Avoidability,"

> I have pointed out that ethical statements are used to influence people, that they change or intensify people's attitudes, rather than describe what these attitudes already are. The influence is mediated not by some occult property which the ethical terms mean, but simply by their *emotive* meaning, which fits them for use in suggestion.[5]

---

[5]Charles L. Stevenson, "Ethical Judgments and Avoidability," *Mind*, Vol. 37 (January 1938), pp. 47–57.

Or, more briefly, the major use of ethical judgments is not to indicate facts, but to create an influence.

It is clear that this function is not *unique* to moral judgments; television commercials, bribes, threats, and presidential debates are also intended to influence attitudes. It is also clear that it is not *essential* to moral judgments, which may be perfectly and intelligently expressed in contexts which one knows one will not influence any attitudes at all.

Geoffrey Warnock seems right on target when he says,

> The fact is that expressing and appealing to the feelings is inci-
> dental to, and actually quite rare in, moral discourse, much as
> exerting influence is incidental to, and quite absent from, mak-
> ing moral judgments. "It would be monstrous to do that!"
> expresses my feelings and may stimulate yours; but "It would be
> wrong to do that" is most unlikely to do either. It expresses an
> opinion, not a state of emotional excitement; it gives you, per-
> haps, my advice against doing something, not a stimulus
> towards emotional revulsion toward doing it. There is nothing,
> in short, *emotive* about moral criticism or approval; moral
> advice may be given in entirely dispassionate terms. Equally, of
> course, a piece of discourse may be highly emotive but uncon-
> cerned with morals; and one's feelings may quite well run
> counter to one's moral views.[6]

It is worth adding that if the essential purpose of a moral judg-
ment is to influence attitudes, then presumably the appropriate criterion for assessing a moral judgment is its degree of success in achieving its purpose. If A's judgment that *Torture for plea-
sure is admirable* influences A's audience to approve torture, and B's judgment that *Torture for pleasure is heinous* does not, then presumably the former judgment is better on the only criterion that fits the case. The same consideration holds for moral arguments. As Warnock notes, for the emotivist "a moral 'argument' . . . might produce its effect or fail to do so, but

---

[6]Geoffrey Warnock, *Philosophy*, p. 27.

there was no room for consideration, as a *further question*, as to whether it was a good argument or a bad one."[7]

The emotivists were caught up in a dilemma. They could identify attitudes with feelings—disapproval of taking human life would then amount merely to feeling negatively toward it, and feeling negatively toward it would then be tantamount to finding it against one's tastes, and about tastes rational persons do not bother to dispute. So much for actual moral disagreement. Or they could emphasize that to hold an attitude involves having a belief—for example, if, say, one approves of increasing Social Security benefits, one believes that persons on Social Security need more money in order to live decently, and this belief is either true or false and is accessible to evidence. An attitude toward X will be appropriate or not depending on whether or not the beliefs relevant to it are true, or at least reasonably held. And then we will be on the verge, at least, of ethical rationalism again.

Prescriptivism

Once the earliest emotivists—Rudolf Carnap, for example— had (as they thought) disposed of ethical rationalism, they seemed not deeply interested in discerning the exact status of alleged moral claims. Carnap suggested that perhaps they were disguised commands. R. M. Hare puts heart and mind into this suggestion, and the result is prescriptivism. A prescription, simply put, is an imperative—a command, an order. No doubt a moral judgment may contain a descriptive component. When A says to B, "Jones is an honest man," what A says entails, "It is characteristic of Jones not to say what is false with intent to deceive." But also, according to Hare, A is telling B to be honest; A is saying to B something like "Become an honest person!" or "Continue in your commendable honesty!" or the like, depending on where A supposes B stands in regard to

---

[7]*Ibid.*, p. 28.

being honest. Hare writes in *The Language of Morals*, "The reason why actions are in a peculiar way revelatory of moral principles is that the function of moral principles is to guide conduct. The language of morals is one sort of prescriptive language . . . although it is no part of my purpose to 'reduce' moral language to imperatives, the study of imperatives is by far the best introduction to the study of ethics."[8] It is Hare's view that "principles of conduct entail particular commands. The entailment is rigorous."[9] The paradigm moral question is, "What shall I do?," and the paradigm moral answer must issue in a moral judgment which, in turn, entails an imperative or command which answers that question. By its nature, morality is action-guiding.

Imperatives, though, may be whimsical or even evil. Asked, "What shall I do?", one can, after all, give a command that is silly or one that it would be wicked to obey. It is only *universalizable* imperatives, Hare holds, that follow from moral judgments. As Warnock puts it:

Such a judgment as "You ought to repay the money" is . . . universalisable; that is, if I commit myself to this judgment in your particular case, I thereby commit myself to the view that anybody — including, most importantly, myself — in the circumstances in which you now are ought to act in that way. I cannot, without logical impropriety, issue a different judgment in another case, unless I can show that other case to be different in some relevant respect. Or if I judge differently some other case which I cannot show to be relevantly different, then I am bound to correct or withdraw my original judgment.[10]

A further feature of imperatives was important for Hare. The indicative sentence, "You are telling the truth," is *true* if and only if you are sticking to the truth; otherwise, it is *false*. The

[8]R. M. Hare, *The Language of Morals* (Oxford: Clarendon Press, 1952) pp. 1–2.

[9]*Ibid.*, p. 55.

[10]Warnock, *Philosophy*, p. 10.

imperative, "tell the truth," is *satisfied* if and only if you tell the truth, and *unsatisfied* otherwise. *Satisfied* and *true*, and *unsatisfied* and *false*, are then supposed to be sufficiently similar to provide something sufficiently like *truth value* for imperatives so that it makes sense to speak of imperatives being entailed by indicative statements.

It should be noted that even if one grants that a person's moral principles are best learned by observing his actions, it does not follow that moral claims entail imperatives. Again, Warnock says it well:

> Thus, from the fact, if it be a fact, that a man's moral principles are revealed most decisively in his behaviour, it does not follow in the least that those principles have to be conceived as, or as implying, *prescriptions*. They might, so far as that point goes, equally well be conceived as expressions of taste or of approval, as avowals of wants or aims, as views about values or ideals, as resolutions, as beliefs about interests, and in many other ways too. On this score at any rate, "Eating people is wrong" is no more closely akin to "Don't eat people" than it is to "I don't want people to be eaten"; for in each of these cases the eating of people, or looking on complacently while people are eaten, would be in some sort of conflict with, even in a sense would contradict, what is said. Why then should we, having conceded, as we must, that moral judgments in general *are* not imperatives, still maintain that they are all in this respect *like* imperatives, that their relation to conduct is to be explained in the same way?[11]

Indeed, there is no *one* way in which moral discourse relates to conduct.

One apparently attractive feature of prescriptionism is that it seems to make room for moral reasoning. One making a moral judgment must — as a point of logic, not morality — be willing to univeralize it; otherwise, the judgment is not a moral judgment at all. If I believe you ought to pay your debts, and can point to

---

[11]*Ibid.*, p. 39.

no relevant difference between us (I am not bankrupt, for example), then I am committed to admit that I ought to pay mine. Of course, as Hare admits, there may be fanatics—people who think that all Jews, or blacks, or women, are morally inferior and should be denied full rights of citizenship and who (usually from the safe assurances of being Gentile, white, or male) grant that *if* they were Jewish, black or female, then they themselves should be denied such rights. One might even find an apparently Gentile Nazi who, upon discovering that he was really mainly Jewish, insists that he be exterminated. But usually people at least formally grant that they are unwilling to be treated unjustly and so ought not to treat others unjustly, even if they quietly continue to do so. What is crucial about Hare's view of the scope of moral argument is that it is limited to considerations of consistency. If I hold that taking the life of males 6 feet or over is morally obligatory, and—upon learning that I qualify—change my view so that it applies only to males at least 7 feet tall, I am inconsistent (and so morally culpable). But if—upon learning that I qualify—I meekly arrange for my own execution, I am a "fanatic" but apparently, on Hare's terms, I do nothing wrong and my moral principle, such as it is, is not inferior to its competitors by being less true or less properly accepted.

Utilitarianism

It is not true, of course, that there was *no* actual moral theory in mid-twentieth-century analytic philosophy. It is true that most of what there was was utilitarian. Invented by Jeremy Bentham, refined by John Stuart Mill, developed further by Henry Sidgwick, and recommended by G. E. Moore, utilitarianism came to dominate philosophical ethics. The utilitarian position, as I shall understand it here, is defined by its acceptance of two claims. One is the *utility principle* which says that an action by an agent on some particular occasion is right if and only if, of all actions open to the agent on that occasion, it produces the greatest balance of good over evil in the long run for the majority of those affected by the action.

Mill claimed certain virtues for utilitarianism. It is, he claimed, the morality of common sense — the one we use anyway, whatever we may say to the contrary. Further, he said, it is compatible with any theology or metaphysic — an attractive feature in a pluralistic society such as ours, one might add. He added that it possesses the advantage that since it includes only one basic moral principle, there cannot be a conflict of moral principles as might occur in an ethical system that contained at least two basic principles.

The other claim essential to utilitarianism is the principle of commensurability, which says that if two things A and B have value, then there is some common coin of measurement in terms of which both A's value and B's can be measured, with no exceptions allowed. If there is value in a taste of peppermint, an understanding of Kant, and the worship of God, then there is a unit of value in terms of which these values, however divergent they may seem or be, can be stated. One can refine and restrict this thesis. One can try to say what the value units are and how they are discerned (this is what Bentham's hedonic calculus, which Mill wisely avoided, attempted to do). One can restrict the thesis to *moral* values and provide some suggestions about how moral values are to be distinguished from other values (economic, aesthetic, religious, or whatever). But such refinement and restriction is irrelevant to what I will say here.

The attractiveness that a utilitarianism comprised of the utility principle and the principle of commensurability possesses for a culture in which computers and cost–benefit analysis play an important role is very great. Nothing I say here is, or is intended as, an attack on computers or on cost–benefit analysis, the benefits of which I do not dispute. But a particular way in which their presence in our society is linked with utilitarianism is neither necessary nor justifiable.

Once one makes the assumption that utilitarianism and cost–benefit analysis are to be wed, the units that cost–benefit analysis measures become the units that provide the common coin for values. Cost-benefit analysis, I said, is neither necessary nor justified. If in circumstances in which there are scarce financial resources and no way to provide free medical services, one takes cost into consideration in making decisions concerning health care. This may simply be a mark of responsibility; it certainly does not mean that one must pretend to weigh the value of human life in monetary terms. So using cost-benefit analysis in order to determine matters which are relevant to moral decisions does not make one a utilitarian. Nor is it unique to utilitarianism to take account of the consequences of actions—any sensible moral theory will involve doing that.

It is sometimes suggested that unless one uses some quantifiable method, rational decision is impossible, but this too is false. I need not be able to quantify the value of both my pen and my wife in order to know which I ought to save from a fire or which it would be wrong to sell.

In fact, utilitarianism possesses none of the advantages that Mill alleged on its behalf. Regarding its alleged common-sense use, consider the wonderfully candid comment by Alan Donagan in *The Theory of Morality*:

> Utilitarians sometimes attempt to show that the calculations their theory calls for are neither as complex nor as difficult as their critics make out. Yet what ought to astonish readers of their work is neither the complexity nor the difficulty of utilitarian calculations, but their absence.[12]

It is seldom if ever clear how one would actually *do* utilitarian moral reasoning.

Regarding the claim that the utility principle serves as an adequate *single* moral principle, consider a case in which the action that will bring about the greatest balance of good over evil for the majority affected in the long run will also distribute that good inequitably. Then justice will require that utility be violated. Hence the utility principle does not (contrary to what

---

[12]Alan Donagan, *The Theory of Morality* (Chicago: University of Chicago Press, 1977), p. 203.

Mill also claims) include a principle of justice. Yet a principle of justice is at least as strong a claimant to the status of being a basic moral principle as is the utility principle itself. It may seem that since each person's interest is counted when a utilitarian allegedly totes up the utility totals, this guarantees justice, but it does not; what would guarantee that would be the requirement that the good be equitably *distributed*, and to add that would be tantamount to adding a principle of justice to the principle of utility as a second basic moral principle. Alone, then, the utility principle is an inadequate basis for morality; supplemented by a principle of justice, it is not the single moral principle. (Utilitarianism's alleged metaphysical neutrality is also bogus, and I will discuss it shortly.)

Utilitarianism has been powerfully criticized in very recent Anglo-American moral philosophy. Bernard Williams's *Morality* and his contribution to *Utilitarianism: For and Against* (co-authored by Williams and J. J. C. Smart) provide an important part of this critique; so do Charles Fried, *Right and Wrong* and Downie and Telfer, *Respect for Persons*. Two points must suffice here.

First, given the commensurability principle, enough trivial goods will outweigh what really matters morally. (Any problem about how many trivial goods are needed is itself a problem for those who pretend there must be moral equations if there is moral rationality.) A human life is outweighed in value by enough tastes of peppermint, provided both have value. No action is unthinkable, for "proper" calculation may support it; nor can infinite value be assigned to some values, for that would ruin commensurability.

Second, as noted, an unjust distribution of goods may result from what is (if anything can be) a correct application of the utility principle. This fact suggests the following model. Suppose that if person A undertakes a certain action, benefits will outweigh costs on utilitarian grounds. The same goes, let us suppose, if B undertakes the same sort of action, though if *both* A and B so act, costs will outweigh benefits. A can argue: if I do X, good outweighs bad (and suppose nothing else A might do instead would so maximize goodness); so, as a good utilitarian, I ought to do X. B can argue exactly analogously. But if A and B both do X, then costs outweigh benefits for both A and B. (There are plenty of real-world cases that will fit this model; an easy example is provided by two equally deserving owners of paper mills either of whose mills may pollute a river to the general benefit but whose collective pollution will poison the river [and so the local water source.])

Utilitarianism, we are often told, breaks here into two kinds. Act-utilitarianism judges individual actions — these are its candidates for basic moral assessment. Rule-utilitarianism judges classes of actions, or practices — given that the practice of doing X will have costs that outweigh its benefits, it is wrong to do X, wrong for anyone to do it. The question here, it seems to me, is not whether it is more rational to consider the practice of X-doing rather than merely the results of A alone doing X, and the results of B alone doing X; the results of one individual doing X, plus the results of one other individual doing X. Each case being considered only in terms of distributive or individual consequences, will not, when added up, yield the actual collective consequence of doing X. Rule-utilitarian procedure makes the better sense; it will yield the more realistic picture.

But is it still utilitarianism that one gets when one proceeds in this fashion? If utilitarianism is comprised by one moral principle — the utility principle — plus (as a claim about all values that is not itself a *moral* principle) the commensurability principle, then the reasoning of the rule-utilitarian (who intends really to be a utilitarian) seems to me most unpromising. Moral rules serve at the pleasure of the utility principle; no moral rule is exceptionless — only the utility principle is exceptionless. So consider the rule-utilitarian's moral rule to the effect that (since the practice of doing X will have more costs than benefits) *One ought not to do X*. A, as a good utilitarian, knows that *his* doing X will have benefits that outweigh costs. His duty is to maximize goodness, and that (as we saw) involves doing X. So he ought to do X, and if he does not, he is an unfaithful utilitarian. The same goes for B. (And there goes the river as a safe water source.)

The so-called rule-utilitarian places a rule *over* the utility principle (and so stops being a utilitarian) or else applies the utility principle directly to A's doing X (and so stops being a *rule*-utilitarian). (J. J. C. Smart makes this sort of point quite effectively in the book, referred to above, that he and Bernard Williams co-authored[13] — each writing his own distinct portions which are antithetical to the other author's sections. Smart refers to the rule-utilitarian as a "rule-worshipper," and so, I think, must a consistent rule-utilitarian appear to an act-utilitarian, who seems to me to be the only really consistent utilitarian.)

What has happened is that the rule-utilitarian has imported a principle of justice which says that if it is not right that everyone do X, then it is not right that anyone do X. This introduces questions about how exactly this principle should be formulated, and with what qualifications, and how this principle is related to the utility principle, and so on. But, strictly speaking, this is not simon-pure utilitarianism with just the utility principle as its only moral principle. An important further element has been introduced. Something of simon-pure utilitarianism has been retained, but something has been rejected (absolute parsimony of moral principles) as something (a principle of justice or moral consistency) has been imported. With the import, utilitarianism (simon-pure variety) has been abandoned, perhaps with gain. Without the import, both A and B ought to do X, even though (on utilitarian grounds — assuming one could tell on such grounds) the effects of their both doing A will be morally worse than would obtain if it was not the case that both did A.

---

[13]J. J. C. Smart and Bernard Williams, *Utilitarianism: For and Against* (Cambridge: Cambridge University Press, 1973).

Renewed Ethical Rationalism

The result of the rejection of emotivism and prescriptivism within most of the Anglo-American ethical tradition, and the recent powerful critique of utilitarianism, has been the revival of perspectives in moral philosophy which are significantly continuous with non-utilitarian traditional ethical rationalism.

I give one example of renewed ethical rationalism, Alan Donagan's *The Theory of Morality*, where Donagan offers as the single moral principle that *it is impermissible not to respect every human being, oneself or any other, as a rational creature.* Obviously, the meaning of this principle will require explanation, and much of *The Theory of Morality* can be seen as clarifying it. Since, for example, to kill another human being *merely at will* is not to respect that person as a rational creature, killing at will is morally impermissible. But it does not follow that killing in self-defense, or defense of one's family, is impermissible. It may be that there are ways in which one can on occasion forfeit one's right to be respected.

Donagan views the moral principle just noted as simply another way of putting one formulation of Kant's categorical imperative — *One ought always to treat persons as ends, and never as means only* or *Rational nature ought always to be respected*. One standard objection to Kant's (and so also to Donagan's) basic moral principle — to put it in Ross's formulation — is to the effect that "ends . . . in the ordinary sense, men are not. For an end is an object of desire, and an object of desire is something that does not yet exist." An end is something we act to bring about; what we act to bring about does not yet exist; but that can hardly be the point of morality. Kant did not see this. So, bluntly put, the objection goes.

Sometimes, in philosophy as without, something passes as profound and unanswerable which is only shallow. Donagan's response to the standard objection to Kant, which objection is neither profound nor unanswerable, deserves to be quoted in full.

Far from embarrassing Kant, it is more probable that such cavils would have astonished him. Nor do I think he would easily have been persuaded that, among Sidgwick's and Ross's countrymen, the belief that the ultimate end of an action is the existing being for whose sake it is done was any less common that it was among his own.

For this familiar conception he might, indeed, have invoked theological authority. "[T]he ultimate end of any maker, as a maker, is himself." Aquinas wrote: "We use things made by us for our own sakes, and if sometimes a man makes a thing for some other purpose, this is referred to his own good, as either useful, or delectable, or fitting [*honestum*]." Obviously, a man who makes things for his own use or pleasure does so ultimately for his own sake; but even when he does something as "fitting," for example, when he observes the terms of his contract with his employer, Aquinas held that he does so as due to himself as well as to his employer. Nor should it be forgotten that not all actions are primarily directed to the use or pleasure of the being who is their ultimate end. This is most evident in actions whose ultimate end is God; for, since God is perfect, nothing anybody does can benefit him in any way at all. "God is the end of things," Aquinas explained, "not in the sense of something set up, or produced, by things, nor in the sense that something is added to him by things, but in this sense only, that he is attained by things." Nor are actions done for the sake of a human being, oneself or another, necessarily or always directed to that person's use or pleasure. The most commonplace examples are acts of courtesy, which may well neither be useful nor pleasing, nor believed to be, but be done and accepted wholly out of mutual respect. Actions of abstaining from injuring or offending others are also of this kind: they are neither pleasing nor useful (for refraining from harming somebody does him no good); but they are morally obligatory, as done out of respect for an already existing being whom practical reason recognizes as an end in itself.[14]

Another objection is that neither "rational nature" nor "person" nor "the proper range of respect for persons" is a very clear

[14]Donagan, *Morality*, pp. 63–64.

notion. This, of course, is correct. Neither is "black hole" nor "quark" nor for that matter "successor of one" a clear notion, independent of their having been clearly explicated. Citing case after case from traditional Judeo-Christian and Greek and Stoic and Modern philosophical and moral discussions, Donagan explores the consequences and applications of his basic moral principle; only in this way is clear content given to such terms as "the proper range of respect for persons." Similarly, though less thoroughly since his is a book on ethics rather than metaphysics, he gives some consideration to the notion of a person, and particularly to the notion of an *agent* and the sort of causality agents must be viewed as possessing. Still, surely there is a degree to which we know quite well what it is to treat a person with respect. It would be odd indeed to insist that to treat a person with respect involved kicking him senseless, or subjecting him to ridicule, or robbing him of even what he needed for sustenance, or brainwashing him. It would be odd indeed to suggest that being another's friend, or engaging with another in a worthwhile project both of you enjoyed and valued and which required your common toil and similar contributions of abilities, or anonymously providing for another's maintenance through a period of crisis, were ways of expressing disrespect for the other person. A group of children would not be paralyzed by an assignment asking them to list ten ways of showing respect, and ten ways of showing disrespect, to their peers. If a philosopher cannot do likewise, it seems unlikely that the explanation is his possession of greater wisdom.

Donagan favors such formulations of his (and Kant's) basic moral principle as those given above to another sort of formulation of a not altogether dissimilar position favored by Aquinas, who preferred some such principle as *Act so that the fundamental human goods, whether in your own person or in that of another, are promoted as may be possible, and in no circumstances violated.* The basic problem with Aquinas's formulation of what he proposes as a basic moral principle from a perspective in many ways empathetic to Kant's and Donagan's is this: it places the primary locus of moral value, not strictly in persons, but in "fundamental human goods," such as health or wisdom. But it is not health, but persons, that possess basic moral worth; and if *being healthy* or *being wise* is valuable, it is because such states fulfill distinctive personal potentials or realize distinctively personal capacities of positive sorts. Hence Kant's or Donagan's formulations, which find in persons the prime locus of moral worth, are superior.

A similar point should be noticed concerning Mill and his utility principle, which places the primary or basic locus of value not in persons, but in certain conscious or psychological states, thus making a mistake somewhat similar to that of Aquinas. This, of course, belies the alleged perfect metaphysical neutrality of Millian utilitarianism.

Space forbids more than mention of another moral philosopher whose word is refreshingly rich and displays deep continuities with traditional moral philosophy, namely Mary Midgley, whose *Beast and Man, Heart and Mind*, and *Wickedness: A Philosophical Essay* (a topic that until recently simply did not appear in polite ethical circles) are too rich a source of moral philosophy to pass by without explicit mention.

Conclusion

The positivistic rejection of ethical rationalism—in both its cultural and intellectual roots and its particular philosophical content—was rationally inadequate. Thus ethics revived. But its late-century version is rather more substantial than its early-century variety. Why?

One reason is its willingness to again relate morality to human nature and the nature of the world. Theories of ethics need theories of human nature and of the larger human environment; morality, if uninhibited by failure of nerve, rubs shoulders with metaphysics and religion. Such authors as Donagan and Midgley do not try to prevent this. A concern to be knowledgeable about, and fair to, what the natural sciences tell us about human nature and the world is part of the same breadth and depth of interest. One need not accept a reduction-ist theory of human nature (a theory that says that a human being is nothing more than a complex organism) or a scientistic epistemology (a theory that says that nothing can be known unless it is learned by application of scientific methods) in order to profit from scientific studies of human capacities.

Another factor is a deep sense of continuity with the philo-sophical tradition. It is no mark of intellectual slavery or lack of originality to interact in depth with the great minds of Euro-pean culture. Donagan and Midgley do this. This is no mere matter of the names or doctrines of traditional philosophers appearing on the pages of their texts; it is rather that they criticize and stretch and revise as well as expound Aristotle or Aquinas or Kant. There is not a distancing from, but rather a critical interaction with, the philosophical tradition.

Still another factor is deep reflection on the Judeo-Christian tradition. For one thing, this helps to prevent Donagan and Midgley from taking a shallow view of evil. It also helps them to resist being overwhelmed by the dark side of nature and of human life. It adds to their realism about what persons are and what they can become. Neither wrote from a religious perspec-tive. Donagan wrote as an agnostic, studying the moral tradi-tion of a Judeo-Christian tradition neither half of which was his own. His conversion to Christianity came only after the book was written. Midgley, so far as I know, neither stands within Judaism or Christianity nor is concerned to contend against those who do. So one has two examples of fine moral philoso-phers who found the Judeo-Christian tradition to be of great relevance to their work without themselves accepting that tradi-tion. Their testimony to its moral depth came, so to speak, from the outside.

Yet another factor is the pleasant fact that real and often complex moral problems are dealt with in the volumes men-tioned. Genuine moral problems are not unmentionables. This feature, no doubt, is a function of those already mentioned.

One final point. Donagan believes that "his" system of moral-ity is in fact the morality of our common humanity, discernible by reflection alone and requiring no theological or religious assumptions. Whether he is right about this is a complex and difficult matter. But even if he is right, much of the point of those who (sometimes against much ridicule) have claimed that you cannot have morality without religion will also be right. For (as Donagan allows, and indeed insists) his theory of morality requires a theory of human nature and — in the long run — a metaphysic (or, perhaps, one or another instance of a *type* of metaphysical system). Much of the point of those who have contended that you cannot have morality without religion has been that you cannot have morality without a theory of human nature and view of the cosmos — in sum, without metaphysics. Much of recent Anglo-American moral philosophy has joined the majority tradition of European ethics in granting that if metaphysics without ethics is vapid, ethics without metaphysics is vacuous. If the Anglo-American moral philosophy done in the remainder of this century continues in the sort of tradition represented by Donagan and Midgley, among others, the prospect of Anglo-American ethics is far more encouraging than its retrospect.

Political-Economic Freedom
and the Biblical Ethic

Ronald H. Nash

Dr. Ronald H. Nash has been head of the department of philosophy and religion at Western Kentucky University since 1966. He has also taught at Barrington College, Houghton College, and Syracuse University. He received his B.A. in philosophy and religion (1958) from Barrington College; his M.A. in philosophy (1960) from Brown University; and his Ph.D. in philosophy from Syracuse University (1964). He has also pursued post-doctoral studies with a grant from the Carnegie Foundation and, at Stanford University, additional post-doctoral work with a grant from the National Endowment for the Humanities. Dr. Nash has published twelve books, including *The New Evangelicalism* (1963); *The Concept of God* (1963); and *Liberation Theology* (1984). He is a member of the Board of Directors of the Institute for Advanced Christian Studies; a consultant on more than fifty fellowship applications to the Institute for Advanced Christian Studies; and a consultant to the Oxford University Press on manuscripts.

Christians have an obligation to see that all their beliefs and actions are consistent with their ultimate religious authority. The magnitude of this duty increases in proportion to the importance of the subject. My talk is an exploration of the biblical ground for my own economic and political convictions. I hold to a political-economic system in which limited government and free-market economics are linked to Judeo-Christian morality. For someone like myself, therefore, it is important that I ask what, if anything, the Bible has to say about limited government and the free market. In the choice between capitalism and socialism, what decision should a biblically informed Christian make?

My general subject is made even more relevant by some recent developments in Christian thinking about society. Within the Christian church today, one can find a small but growing army of Protestants and Roman Catholics who have entered into an uncritical alliance with the political Left.[1] By now, most of us have heard about the so-called liberation theologians who not only promote a synthesis of Marxism and Christianity but who attempt to ground their recommended restrictions of economic and political freedom on their interpretation of the biblical ethic. A growing number of my own religious fellowship (those theologically conservative Protestants known as evangelicals) appear to stop just short of the more radical pronouncements of the liberation thinkers. Nonetheless, these liberal (or in some cases radical) evangelicals hold views of society that certainly have the writings of Marx as one of their major sources. In many Christian colleges and seminaries, the course title "Social Ethics" is often just a euphemism for "Socialist Ethics." These evangelicals of the Left are convinced that the biblical ethic obliges them to condemn capitalism and endorse the politics of statism and the economics of socialism.

The confusing of the Christian Gospel with the politics and economics of collectivism is apparent in a recent public statement from a group of Canadian bishops. Economist Paul Heyne's comments about the bishop's views are instructive:

> To put it simply, the bishops are rejecting, in the name of Gospel principles, any economic system coordinated by changing relative money prices. For in any such system, people will necessarily be treated impersonally (in some respects), important decisions will be made (within legal and moral constraints) by the criterion of net return on capital, and human wants or needs will (to a large extent) be satisfied only insofar as they express themselves through money bids. The bishops are predisposed to

[1] I am equally disappointed by any who enter into an *uncritical* alliance with the political Right.

believe that this system *does not work*, and hence ready to sub-
scribe to a Marxist analysis of its effects, because they are deeply
convinced, on ethical grounds, that it *should not exist*. They will
therefore not be easily persuaded that *only* such a system has the
capability of feeding, clothing, housing, and otherwise caring
for large populations in a manner even remotely close to what
almost all Canadians now expect as a matter of right.[2]

There is a lot of confusion with the Christian Left. I do not
want to appear unaware of the major differences that often
separate those whose guru is George McGovern from those who
regard Karl Marx as a crypto-Christian. But at the same time,
the complexity of my subject and the limited space at my disposal will not always allow me to make all the fine distinctions
that I might like.[3]

Since my subject is so large, let me mention some things that I
will not be able to cover. I am going to say relatively little about
political freedom. For one thing, I don't have time to write
about everything. Moreover, the people with whom I disagree
seldom express their opposition to political freedom explicitly.
No one that I know is digging through the Bible seeking proof
texts that support totalitarianism. The Christians on the Left
give lip service to democracy. But, of course, the extent to
which their economic collectivism may reduce or even destroy
political freedom is another matter. The more extreme Leftists
recognize the restraints on political freedom that will be necessary whenever their proposals are first put into effect. Like all
Marxist utopians, they look forward to a day when the new
social structures will transform human nature and political
coercion can end. Lenin offered the Russian people the same
false hope. Anyway, I will say relatively little about political

---

[2]The text of the Canadian bishops' statement, along with several discussions
of the text, can be found in "Economics and the Canadian Bishops: A
Symposium," *This World*, 5 (Spring/Summer, 1983), 122–145. The quote
from Heyne appears on p. 140.

[3]I do make many of these distinctions in my book, *Social Justice and the
Christian Church* (Milford, Michigan: Mott, 1983).

freedom.[4] Most of my remarks will be directed to the question of economic freedom.

What is the most promising way for a Christian to go about relating his economic convictions to the Bible? Many writings from the Christian Left illustrate what can be called the proof-text method. What these writers normally do is isolate some vague passage (usually one from the Old Testament) that pertains to an extinct cultural situation or practice. They then proceed to deduce some complex economic or political program from that text. My book, *Social Justice and the Christian Church*, refers to several examples of this procedures.[5] What these writers really do, of course, is manipulate the Bible for their own secular ends. They just read their own pet twentieth-century secular theory into a portion of the Word of God that they have torn from its biblical and cultural context. Attempts to deduce any political or economic doctrine from the Bible should be viewed, initially at least, with skepticism. After all, the Bible is no more a textbook on economics than it is on astronomy or geology. Some parts of the Old Testament contain instructions that were intended for limited situations and limited periods of time.

My own approach is different. In my view, Christians are required to believe many things, not because they are taught *explicitly* in the Bible, but *simply because they are true*! Every

---

[4]In this connection, it is relevant to add a reminder of the conservative conviction that economic freedom and political-spiritual freedom are a whole that cannot be divided. Freedom is indivisible. As Wilhelm Roepke saw so clearly, "We are not free to combine just any kind of economic order, say, a collectivist one, with any kind of political and spiritual order." *A Humane Economy* (Indianapolis: Liberty Fund, 1971), p. 105. Economics is not simply a matter of finding the most expedient way to organize economic life. There is a necessary connection between economic freedom and political-spiritual freedom. Because liberty is an indivisible whole, it is impossible to have political and spiritual freedom without also having economic freedom. Because collectivism in the economic sphere means the end of political and spiritual freedom, economics is the front line in the battle for freedom.

[5]*Social Justice*, op. cit., ch. 6.

sensible Christian believes many things that are not explicitly taught in Scripture. He holds them because they are true; and because they *are* true, the propositions will be consistent with what Scripture teaches.

My approach to the subject rejects the proof-text method and proceeds via three main steps. First, a Christian should acquire a clear and complete picture of the Christian world view. What basic views about God, humankind, morality and society are taught or implied by Scripture? Then he should put his best effort into discovering the truth about economic and political systems. He should try to clarify what capitalism and socialism really are (not what the propagandists say they are); he should try to discover how each system works or, as in the case of socialism, whether it can work. He should identify the strengths and weaknesses of each system. He should compare his economic options to the standard of biblical morality. Entirely too many sincere but confused Christians of late have rushed to make pronouncements about complex social, economic and political issues without first taking the time to become informed about these subjects. Many writings of Christian social activists evidence an inadequate grasp of economics.[6] It is not enough to feel compassion for poor and oppressed people. Compassion and love must be coupled with a careful grounding in the relevant philosophical, economic and political issues. When proposals to help the poor are grounded on bad economics, they will usually make any bad situation worse.

To repeat the three steps of my approach: in step one, we should first formulate carefully a well-rounded Christian world view. In step two, we should do the best we can to discover the truth about competing economic and political systems. Step three: After we know what we're talking about, we should compare these systems to the biblical view of God, man, morality and society and ask which system is more consistent with the entire Christian world view. Which system—capitalism or socialism—should I as a *thinking* Christian choose? Of course,

---

[6]For some examples, see my book, *Social Justice and the Christian Church*.

some of my Christian friends on the Left think that this is exactly what they have done. But as I have argued elsewhere, they are wrong.[7] Their writings make it clear that the capitalism they oppose is a caricature and the socialism they recommend is pure fantasy.

Some Relevant Aspects of the Biblical World View

I must be very selective here because of my need to be brief.

(1) Certainly the biblical world view implies that since God is the creator of all that exists, He ultimately is the rightful owner of all that exists. Whatever possessions a human being may acquire, he holds them temporarily as a steward of God and is ultimately accountable to God for how he uses them. However omnipresent greed and avarice may be in the human race, they are clearly incompatible with the moral demands of the biblical world view.

(2) The biblical world view also contains important claims about human rights and liberties. All human beings have certain natural rights inherent in their created nature and have certain moral obligations to respect the rights of others. The possibility of human freedom is not a gift of government but a gift from God. Freedom has its ground in our created nature. Man's essential freedom and his right to exercise that freedom are his by virtue of his creation in God's image. But freedom has its limits. As E. David Cook warns:

> We are created beings. We are not free to be whatever we wish to be or would like to be. We are God's creatures and that must imply certain limits as to what man is able to do and to be. . . . Is man free to make his own laws and to live his life in any way he pleases? The Christian answer must be negative. Man may try to

---

[7]In addition to *Social Justice and the Christian Church* (already cited), see Ronald Nash, *Freedom, Justice and the State* (Lanham, Maryland: University Press of America, 1980), and Ronald Nash, ed., *Liberation Theology* (Milford, Michigan: Mott, 1984).

live without reference to God and even try to assume responsibility for himself, but he cannot escape from his maker and his created being. He does not have infinite possibilities for change bound up in himself. Man is limited.[8]

In the Old Testament, freedom is contrasted with slavery. The opposite of freedom is servitude and constraint, being forced to do the will of another (Ex. 21:2-11; Isa. 61:1; Jer. 34:14-17). So the Old Testament tended to focus on the economic and social dimensions of freedom. But gradually, as one moves into the New Testament, a more spiritual dimension of freedom assumes dominance. Human beings lack freedom, not just because they are slaves to the will of another human being, but because they are slaves to sin (Rom. 7:14; 6:17-20; 2 Cor. 3:17). The apostle Paul connected true freedom with the believer's new relationship with Jesus Christ (Gal. 5:1). In the words of Jesus, "I tell you the truth, everyone who sins is a slave to sin . . . if the Son sets you free, you will be free indeed . . . you will know the truth and the truth will set you free" (John 8:36, 31). Spiritual freedom in the New Testament is deliverance from bondage to sin and is available only to those who come to know God's truth through Christ and enter into the saving relationship with Christ described in the New Testament.

Some interesting parallels between the biblical account of spiritual freedom and political-economic freedom should be noted. For one thing, freedom always has God as its ultimate ground. For another, freedom must always exist in relationship to law. The moral law of God identifies definite limits beyond which human freedom under God should not pass. Liberty should never be turned into license.

(3) The moral system of the Bible is another key element of the Christian world view. While the Ten Commandments do not constitute the entire biblical ethic, they are a good place to

---

[8]E. David Cook, "Man in Society," in *Essays in Evangelical Social Ethics*, David F. Wright, ed. (Wilton, Connecticut: Morehouse-Barlow, 1983), p. 135.

begin. But it is important to notice other dimensions of the biblical ethic that have relevance for our subject. For example, Christians on the Left insist that the biblical ethic condemns individual actions and social structures that oppress people, harm people and favor some at the expense of others (*See* Ez. 34). I agree. Where I disagree, however, is with the next step taken by the Leftists. They claim that capitalism inevitably and necessarily encourages individual actions and produces social structures that oppress and harm people. On this point, they are dead wrong. Fortunately, the question as to which system actually harms or helps different classes of people is an empirical and not a normative matter. The Leftists simply have their facts wrong.[9]

(4) One final aspect of the Christian world view must be mentioned: the inescapable fact of human sin and depravity. No economic or political system that assumes the essential goodness of human nature or holds out the dream of a perfect earthly society can possibly be consistent with the biblical world view.

Our Economic Options

I have taken an all-too-quick look at some relevant aspects of the biblical world view. Now we must examine, again all too briefly, our major economic options. There are three economic systems that compete for attention: capitalism, socialism and somewhere between, the hybrid known as interventionism or the mixed economy. I have argued elsewhere that it is a mistake to regard capitalism, socialism and interventionism as words that denote specific positions.[10] It is best to treat them as umbrella terms that cover a variety of positions along a contin-

---

[9]For support for my claim, see my own three books that have already been cited, along with works cited in their bibliographies.

[10]See Ronald Nash, "The Christian Choice Between Capitalism and Socialism," in *Liberation Theology*, op. cit., pp. 49–67.

uum. One dominant feature of capitalism is economic freedom, the right of people to exchange things voluntarily, free from force, fraud and theft. Capitalism is more than this, of course, but its concern with free exchange is obvious.

Socialism, on the other hand, seeks to replace the freedom of the market with a group of central planners who exercise control over essential market functions. There are degrees of socialism as there are degrees of capitalism in the real world. But basic to any form of socialism is distrust of or contempt for the market process and the desire to replace the freedom of the market with some form of centralized control. Generally speaking, as one moves along the continuum from socialism to capitalism, one finds the following: the more freedom a socialist allows, the closer his position is to interventionism; the more freedom an interventionist allows, the closer his position is to capitalism. It is clear that the real issue in the dispute among these three positions is the degree of economic freedom each allows. The crux is the extent to which human beings will be permitted to exercise their own choices in the economic sphere of life.

I will say nothing more about the deplorable economic system known as interventionism. Ludwig von Mises said it all. Interventionism is a hopeless attempt to stop on a slippery slope where no stop is possible. The only way the half-hearted controls of the interventionist can work is if they become the *total* controls of the socialist. Anything less will result in the kind of failed economy we have in the United States.[11]

I shall attempt to get a clearer fix on the real essence both of capitalism and socialism and then see which is more compatible with the biblical world view. The best starting point for this comparison is a distinction made most recently by the American economist, Walter Williams. According to Williams, there are two and only two ways in which something may be exchanged. He called them *the peaceful means of exchange* and *the violent*

---

[11]For more, see Nash, *Freedom, Justice and the State*, op. cit., ch. 5.

means of exchange.[12] The peaceful means of exchange may be summed up in the phrase, "If you do something good for me, then I'll do something good for you." When capitalism is understood correctly, it epitomizes the peaceful means of exchange. The reason people exchange in a real market is because they believe the exchange is good for them. They take advantage of an opportunity to obtain something they want more in exchange for something they desire less. Capitalism then should be understood as a voluntary system of relationships that utilizes the peaceful means of exchange.

But exchange can also take place by means of force and violence. In this violent means of exchange, the basic rule of thumb is: "Unless you do something good for me, I'll do something bad to you." This turns out to be the controlling principle of socialism. Socialism means far more than centralized control of the economic process. It entails the introduction of coercion into economic exchange in order to facilitate the attainment of the goals of the elite who function as the central planners. One of the great ironies of Christian socialism is that its proponents in effect demand that the state get out its weapons and force people to fulfill the demands of Christian love. Even if we fail to notice any other contrast between capitalism and socialism, we already have a major difference to relate to the biblical ethic. One system stresses voluntary and peaceful exchange while the other depends on coercion and violence.

Some Christian socialists object to the way I have set this up. They profess contempt for the more coercive forms of state-socialism on exhibit in communist countries. They would like us to believe that a more humane, noncoercive kind of socialism is possible. They would like us to believe that there is a form of socialism, not yet tried anywhere on earth, where the central

---

[12]Some have been troubled by Williams's use of "violence" in this distinction. It may help to note that the word is used in a somewhat technical sense, viz., "the abusive or unjust exercise of power." In many situations, the violence that Williams has in view is implicit. It functions primarily as a threat. As long as one does the state's bidding, the state will not unleash the force it has at its disposal.

ideas are cooperation and community and where coercion and dictatorship are precluded. This is an interesting semantic game. Either these people are confused or they don't want to let the rest of us in on the dirty secret. It is interesting to note how little information they provide about the workings of this more utopian kind of socialism. For another, they simply ignore the fact that however humane and voluntary their socialism is supposed to become after it has been put into effect, it will take massive amounts of coercion and theft to get things started.

But there is another problem. Voluntary socialism is a contradiction in terms. As Edmund Opitz points out, "Such practices as voluntarily pooling goods, sharing the common tasks of a community, working with the hands . . . do not constitute Socialism."[13] What these Christian socialists have done is formed a utopian ideal of a voluntary community and called it socialism. They are unable to explain how their system will work without free markets and they simply ignore the massive amounts of coercion that will be required to get their system started. Whatever else socialism is, it means a centralized control of the economy made possible by the use of force. Socialism epitomizes the violent means of exchange.

The most serious difficulty with socialism—call it socialism's Achilles' heel—is still the problem Ludwig von Mises pointed out back in 1920. Socialism is an economic system that makes economic activity impossible. As Giovanni Sartori explains, under socialism it is "theoretically and practically impossible, for the collectivistic planner, to *calculate costs*. His costs and prices are, and can only be, 'arbitrary.' To be sure, arbitrary not in the sense that they are established at whim but in the sense that they are *baseless*: they cannot be derived from any economically significant base or baseline."[14] Without free markets and the vital information markets supply, economic activ-

---

[13]Edmund Opitz, "Socialism," in *Bakers Dictionary of Christian Ethics*, Carl F. H. Henry, ed. (Grand Rapids: Baker, 1973), p. 639.

[14]Giovanni Sartori, "The Market, Planning, Capitalism and Democracy," *This World*, 5 (Spring/Summer, 1983), 59.

ity would become chaotic and result in drastic inefficiencies and distortions. The great paradox of socialism is the fact that socialists need capitalism in order to survive. Unless socialists make allowance for some free markets which provide the pricing information that alone makes rational economic activity possible or monitor the pricing information available from free markets, socialist economies would have even more problems than those for which they are already notorious. In practice, socialism cannot dispense with market exchanges. Consequently, socialism is a gigantic fraud which attacks the market at the same time it is forced to utilize the market process. Surely, this truth has relevance to the subject before us.

But critics of the market conveniently ignore von Mises' argument and try to shift attention away from their own embarrassing problems to claims that capitalism must be abolished or restricted because it is unjust or because it restricts important human freedoms. Capitalism is supposed to be un-Christian because it allegedly gives a predominant place to greed and other un-Christian values. It is alleged to increase poverty and the misery of the poor while, at the same time, it makes a few rich at the expense of the many. Socialism, on the other hand, is portrayed as the economic system of people who really care for the less fortunate members of society. Socialism is the economics of compassion. Socialism is also recommended on the ground that it encourages other basic Christian values such as community. If these claims were true, they would constitute a serious problem for anyone anxious to show that capitalism is compatible with the biblical ethic. But, of course, the claims are not true. People who make such charges have their facts wrong or are aiming at the wrong target. The "capitalism" they accuse of being inhumane is a caricature. The system that in fact produces the consequences they deplore turns out to be not capitalism, but interventionism.[15]

---

[15]For more on all this, see my *Social Justice and the Christian Church*, op. cit.

A Clearer Vision of the Nature of Capitalism

I have already explained capitalism as a system of voluntary human relationships in which people exchange on the basis of the peaceful means of exchange. Capitalism, however, is not economic anarchy. For one thing, capitalism recognizes several necessary conditions for the kinds of voluntary relationships it recommends. One of these presuppositions is the existence of inherent human rights, such as the right to make decisions, the right to be free, the right to hold property, and the right to exchange what one owns for something else. Capitalism also presupposes a system of morality. Capitalism does not encourage people to do anything they want. There are definite limits, moral and otherwise, to the ways in which humans should exchange. Capitalism should be thought of as a system of voluntary relationships within a framework of laws which protect people's rights against force, fraud, theft and violations of contracts. "Thou shalt not steal" and "Thou shalt not lie" are part of the underlying moral constraints of the system.[16] Economic exchanges can hardly be voluntary if one participant is coerced, deceived, defrauded or robbed.[17]

One of the sillier objections to capitalism is the claim that it presupposes a utopian view of human nature and consequently conflicts with the biblical view of sin. We have already seen who the utopians in this dispute are. My earlier statement about the need for laws to protect people from force, fraud and theft hardly sounds like capitalism is unaware of the true condition of human nature. Once we grant that consistency with the bibli-

---

[16]Compare this with the biblical concern for just weights and measures (Deut. 25:15,16).

[17]I should add that we have a right to expect more than minimal conformity to the spirit and framework of the market system. Christians have a right to expect both buyers and sellers to go the second mile with regard to their ethical obligations. But as we all know, human beings are fallen creatures who can be expected to bend, if not break, the rules when they believe it will be to their advantage. One of the more rapidly growing areas of philosophy is business ethics. It would be interesting to see a business ethics text written by someone committed both to the biblical ethic and to the free market.

cal doctrine of sin is a legitimate test of political and economic systems, it is relatively easy to see how well democratic capitalism scores in this regard. The limited government willed to Americans by the founding fathers was influenced in large measure by biblical considerations about human sin. Because the founding fathers believed that human nature could not be trusted, they created a complicated and cumbersome system of government in which various checks and balances served to make the attainment of absolute power by any one man or group extremely difficult. Such nineteenth-century liberals as John Stuart Mill believed that government should be limited because men are essentially good. But the founding fathers believed that government should be limited because men are essentially evil. If one of the more effective ways of mitigating the effects of human sin in society is dispersing and decentralizing power, the conservative view of government is on the right track. So too is the conservative vision of economics.

The combination of a free-market economy and limited constitutional government is the most effective means yet devised to impede the concentration of economic and political power in the hands of a small number of people. Every person's ultimate protection against coercion requires control over some private spheres of life where he can be free. Private ownership of property is an important buffer against any exorbitant consolidation of power by government. The free market is consistent with the biblical view of human nature in another way. It recognizes the weaknesses of human nature and the limitations of human knowledge. No one can possibly know enough to manage a complex economy. No one should ever be trusted with this power. However, in order for socialism to work, it requires a class of omniscient planners to forecast the future, to set prices, and to control production. In the free-market system, decisions are not made by an omniscient bureaucratic elite but made across the entire economic system by countless economic agents. So once again, when capitalism is understood correctly, it conforms to biblical models of ownership and exchange; it is compatible with the biblical view of human nature.

At this point, of course, collectivists will raise another set of objections. Capitalism, they will counter, may make it difficult for economic power to be consolidated in the hands of the state; but it only makes it easier for vast concentrations of wealth and power to be vested in the hands of private individuals and companies. The point of course is that it is supposed to be capitalism that produces monopolies. But the truth turns out to be something quite different from this widely accepted myth. It is not the free market that produces monopolies; rather it is governmental intervention with the market that creates the conditions that encourage monopoly.[18]

As for another old charge, that capitalism encourages greed, the truth is just the reverse. The mechanism of the market neutralizes greed as selfish individuals are forced to find ways of servicing the needs of those with whom they wish to exchange. As we know, various people often approach economic exchanges with motives and objectives that fall short of the biblical ideal. But no matter how base or selfish a person's motives may be, so long as the rights of the other parties are protected, the greed of the first individual cannot harm them. As long as greedy individuals are prohibited from introducing force, fraud and theft into the exchange process, their greed must be channeled into the discovery of products or services for which people are willing to exchange their holdings. Every person in a market economy has to be other directed. The market is one area of life where concern for the other person is required. The market then does not pander to greed. It is rather a mechanism that allows natural human desires to be satisfied in a nonviolent way. The alternative to the peaceful means of exchange is violence and coercion.[19]

---

[18]See Nash, *Freedom, Justice and the State*, op. cit., pp. 128 ff. and 184 ff.

[19]See my earlier comment on this technical use of the word "violence" in note 12.

Some Other Problems for the Christian Left

I have said enough about the *bad economics* practiced by those who would ground economic collectivism on the Bible. Members of the Christian Left have some other difficulties. One of these is their *bad hermeneutics*.

By hermeneutics, I am referring to the way in which Christians on the Left interpret and use the Bible in support of their political and economic beliefs. Attempts to ground American liberalism and interventionism or Latin American liberationism on the Bible involve serious distortions of the biblical message. What liberation theologians do, for example, is read the Bible through Marxist spectacles. According to theologian Bruce Demarest,

> The Marxist-socialist critique of capitalist society wrongly forms the basis for the liberationist's interpretation of the Word of God. Instead of allowing its vision of the world to be shaped by the teachings of Scripture, liberation theology permits its understanding of Scripture to be shaped by analysis of the existing social order. The Christian's text must be the Word of God rather than the historical situation . . .[20]

Demarest goes on to deplore the extent to which radical Christians use biblical texts "as pretexts to justify pet economic and political theories." Most liberation theologians, for example, "do little more than hang biblical window-dressing on the framework of a sociological theory," a sociological theory incidentally that they derive from Marx.

Even the much less radical American evangelicals on the Left abuse the Bible more than they use it. Often their proof-texts ignore the biblical context. Just as frequently, their appeal to the Bible ignores the cultural context.[21] Moreover, the Leftist's hermeneutics frequently depends on his reading twentieth-

---

[20]Bruce Demarest, *General Revelation* (Grand Rapids: Zondervan, 1982), pp. 214–215.

[21]For examples, see Nash, *Social Justice*, op. cit., ch. 6.

century meanings into ancient Hebrew and Greek terms. A good example of this is the way such Christians on the Left handle the biblical notion of justice. The basic idea in the Old Testament notion of justice is righteousness and fairness. But it is essential to the Leftist's cause that he read into biblical pronouncements about justice, contemporary notions of distributive justice. When the Bible says that Noah was a just man, it does not mean that he would have voted the straight Democratic ticket. It means simply that he was a righteous man.[22]

The bad hermeneutics of the Christian radicals may be one possible explanation for their *bad theology*. Their treatment of Jesus' teaching in Luke 4:16-19 is typical. According to Luke's account, Jesus entered into a synagogue and read from Isaiah 61:1,2: "The Spirit of the Lord is on me, because he has anointed me to preach good news to the poor. He has sent me to proclaim freedom for the prisoners and recovery of sight for the blind, to release the oppressed, to proclaim the year of the Lord's favor." Many Christians on the Left use this text to reinterpret Jesus' earthly mission in exclusively economic and political terms. In their view, Jesus came primarily to deliver those who were poor and oppressed in a material sense.

But the traditional Christian understanding of this text and of Jesus' ministry is quite different. According to the traditional view, the poverty the text has in view is spiritual poverty. Every member of the human race is poor in the sense of being spiritually bankrupt. None of us have any righteousness of our own. All of us are too blind spiritually to see the nature of our problem or the way of deliverance. All of us are oppressed by the chains of sin. Jesus came to deliver us from the power and penalty of sin. He came to give us spiritual sight and to end our spiritual poverty by making available the righteousness that God demands and that only God can provide. To turn the basic message of the Gospel into an apology for political revolution is heresy!

Bad theology that borders on heresy seems to be a trademark

---

[22]For more, see Nash's *Social Justice*, chs. 3 and 6.

of some liberation theologians. Some have blurred the distinction between the church (the company of redeemed believers) and the world. Some have suggested that the poor are saved simply because they are poor. Others imply that God cares more about the poor than he cares about the rich.[23] It is heresy to state that God's love for people varies in proportion to their wealth and social class. It is nonsense to suggest that all the poor are good and all the rich are evil.

The bad economics, bad hermeneutics and bad theology of the Christian Left are quite at home with the *bad consequences* of their kind of approach to social problems. Statist efforts to help the poor and oppressed have been counterproductive and inevitably, it seems, end up increasing the misery of the people the statists supposedly want to help. Liberal housing programs in America have not made more low-cost housing available for the poor; the result has been much less available housing. Minimum-wage legislation does not really help people at the bottom of the economic ladder; it ends up harming them by making them less employable. Regardless of where one looks, the programs of the welfare state have failed. George Gilder points out that liberals who write such glowing reports of all the progress the American poor have supposedly made in their struggle against poverty in the past twenty years have a badly distorted vision of reality.

> What actually happened since 1964 was a vast expansion of the welfare rolls that halted in its tracks an ongoing improvement in the lives of the poor, particularly blacks, and left behind . . . a wreckage of broken lives and families worse than the aftermath of slavery. Although intact black families are doing better than ever, and discrimination has vastly diminished, the condition of poor blacks has radically worsened.[24]

---

[23]I document these charges in ch. 12 of my *Social Justice and the Christian Church.*

[24]George Gilder, *Wealth and Poverty* (New York: Basic, 1981), ch. 1.

It is not conservatism that is inhumane; it is liberal statism. It is not a lack of compassion that leads conservatives to oppose the welfare state and other collectivist measures. On the contrary, it is their compassion plus a decidedly clearer vision of the consequences of welfare state policies that produces their opposition. Addressing the inhumane consequences of American welfare state policies, Warren T. Brookes states that nothing "can begin to match the systematic degradation, dehumanization, and cultural genocide that have been wreaked on black Americans." The American government, he continues, has in the past twenty years, with the best of intentions, "seduced blacks out of the rigors of the marketplace and into the stifling womb of the welfare state." He goes on to cite some troubling statistics:

> In 1962 only one black family in 20 was on welfare. Only one black child in 6 was born to a fatherless home. Black youth employment was at an even higher ratio than that of whites, and youth unemployment for that group was at 10–12 percent, roughly the same as whites.
>   Today, one black family in 5 is on welfare, and 55 percent of all black children were born to unwed mothers last year. Black youth unemployment is 40 percent, nearly triple that of whites, while black employment ratios have actually declined, even as white ratios have soared.[25]

The liberal welfare state is speeding us down the tracks to destruction of the family and the disintegration of society. And it is doing this in the name of compassion. Yet Christians on the Left continue to tell us that what the Bible demands is not less but rather more of this "humanitarian" statism.

Conclusion

Once we eliminate the semantic game-playing by which some refer to a noncoercive voluntary utopian type of socialism, it

---

[25]Warren T. Brookes, "High Technology and Judeo-Christian Values," *Imprimis* (April, 1984).

becomes clear that socialism is incompatible with a truly free society. Edmund Opitz has seen this clearly:

> There are two radically opposed ways of life here: Socialism versus the Free Society, and they lock horns over the questions: Who shall plan? and For Whom? Socialism has an overall plan which the handful of men who wield political power must impose on the mass of citizenry in order that the intended national goals and purposes may be realized. But, millions of people have billions of plans of their own, and because many of these private plans do not fit into the government's plan they must be annulled; and if persuasion does not suffice punishment must be invoked. . . . Socialism means a nation with two kinds of men; the few who have the power to run things and the many whose lives are run by other men.[26]

The people best suited to force others into their plan for society are those controlled by ideology. They see themselves as servants of some great movement as they go about forcing others to conform to their blueprint for society.

> As History's vice-regent, the Planner is forced to view men as mass; which is to deny their full stature as persons with rights endowed by the Creator, gifted with free will, possessing the capacity to order their own lives in terms of their convictions. The man who has the authority and the power to put the masses through their paces, and to punish nonconformists, must be ruthless enough to sacrifice a person to a principle. . . . a commissar who believes that each person is a child of God will eventually yield to a commissar whose ideology is consonant with the demands of his job.[27]

And so, Opitz concludes, "Socialism needs a secular religion to sanction its authoritarian politics, and it replaces the traditional moral order by a code which subordinates the individual to the

---

[26]Opitz, op. cit., pp. 639–40.
[27]*Ibid.*, p. 640.

collective." All of this is justified in the cause of improving economic well-being and in the name of compassion.

I think I have said enough to allow me, at least, to make a reasoned choice between capitalism and socialism on the basis of each system's compatibility to the biblical world view. The alternative to free exchange is violence. Capitalism is a mechanism that allows natural human desires to be satisfied in a nonviolent way. Little can be done to prevent human beings from wanting to be rich. But what capitalism does is channel that desire into peaceful means that benefit many besides those who wish to improve their own situation. As Arthur Shenfield explains, "The alternative to serving other men's wants is seizing power of them, as it always has been. Hence it is not surprising that wherever the enemies of capitalism have prevailed, the result has been not only the debasement of consumption standards for the masses but also their reduction to serfdom by the new privileged class of socialist rulers."[28]

Which choice then should I, as a Christian, make in the selection between capitalism and socialism? Capitalism is quite simply the most moral system, the most effective system, and the most equitable system of economic exchange. When capitalism, the system of free economic exchange, is described fairly, there can be no question that it, rather than socialism or interventionism, comes closer to matching the demands of the biblical ethic.

---

[28]Arthur Shenfield, "Capitalism Under the Tests of Ethics," *Imprimis* (December, 1981).

Market and Money
in Jewish and Christian Thought
in the Hellenistic and Roman Ages

Leonard Liggio

Mr. Leonard P. Liggio is President of the Institute for Humane Studies and the editor of *Literature of Liberty*. He has served as vice president of the Cato Institute, director of the Center for Cultural Diversity, and on the faculties at the City College of New York and the State University of New York at Old Westbury. He has also served as chairman of the Liberty Fund Seminars, 1978–1982, and director of several symposia, including "New Deal Foreign Policy," Gibson Island, Maryland (1971) and West Point (1980). He did his undergraduate work at Georgetown University and pursued graduate studies at Fordham University.

The theme that I'm undertaking is a rather complex one, and its prominence as an issue of debate has arisen only recently, mainly because of the development of liberation theology. If one examines the writings of theologians who have emerged in recent years and who have undertaken to write under the rubric of liberation theology, one finds that they make very extensive references to the Old and New Testaments and to the Fathers of the Church in order to establish a line of legitimacy directly to themselves and to consign their opponents to eternal darkness. Therefore, it is important for us, first of all, to examine what it is that early Christians, and before that the Jewish community, felt about the issues of property and second, to try and understand the context in which the Fathers of the Church were writing so that their teachings on these matters might be properly interpreted.

For us to do an extensive analysis would mean that we would be required to devote a great deal of attention and time to the economy and society of the ancient world—that is, the Oriental empires such as Persia and Egypt; the Hellenistic empires that succeeded Alexander the Great; and their successor, the Roman Empire. None of the teachings of the prophets, Jesus Christ, the Apostles, and the Fathers of the Church are understandable unless one understands the social conditions to which they were addressing themselves. For the most part, liberation theologians ignore the historical situation and simply grab the texts without attempting to place them in the context in which they were written and which, hence, would give them a very different understanding.

If one examines the Old Testament, one finds references, first of all, to issues such as private property. In the earliest books of the Old Testament, when the Jews arrived in the Holy Land, land was distributed to them as individual holdings, and they were enjoined under penalty of sin from moving boundaries from the land or changing the boundaries. That would amount to a form of theft that would ultimately be a form of coveting a neighbor's goods. At the same time, in the writings of the Old Testament, there is a strong line of thought that emphasizes that one should not make an idol of property, just as one should not make an idol of poverty; that none of the issues of goods— having goods or lacking goods—should be made an idol; and that they should not come before one's obligations to religion.

Simultaneously, in the Old Testament there are references to the taking of property unjustly. For example, in Isaiah 1:23 the prophet warns princes not to consort with thieves nor to give corrupt judgments. This is preceded (V. 22) by the statement, "Thy silver has become dross; thy wine has become mixed with water." He is warning there against the dilution of currency, and we see that in many other places in the Old Testament where the prophets are condemning this dilution by the rules (in essence, inflation), and treating it as a major form of theft alongside the latters' taking-away of private property.

Ezekiel (22:18-22) uses the evil of debasing coin as an example for people to address in their individual reformation, so this topic keeps reappearing in the prophetic literature. The debasing of coin is considered similar to debasing one's individual religious activities, an example of sin in itself and as a model for the individual in the reform of his activities.

The Old Testament prophets place great emphasis upon defending the individual family's right of property against the state. Ezekiel warns against oppression whereby the property owned by the individual Jew is taken by the ruler. This is a major theme that then continues in a good deal of the early Christian literature.

Wealth is given, in the Old Testament, to be used productively and wisely, and this theme is continued into the New Testament. In I Timothy 1:3, there is a strong statement about the responsibility of the family to produce and thereby to care for its own. What the Old Testament prophets and some of the writings in the early Church say is actually a defense of the family, and in order to defend the family it is important, in their eyes, to defend private property. Assault on the family through assault on private property is seen as a cause of the decline of religious belief and of the ability of the family to worship properly.

Since the early Church came into existence in the midst of the Hellenistic and Roman period, it is important to know something about the idea of property and wealth as seen by those people, who, in large measure, eventually became Christians. The Greeks and the Romans had a very strong sense of property, parallel to that of the Jews in the Old Testament. For the Greeks and the Romans, there was a strong interconnection among private property, the family, and religion. To them, each family was an individual unit of worshipers and had a direct connection between itself and its god. Therefore, each family had its own place of worship in its home, and the home and the surroundings—property—was sacred to that family. No one could violate private property because that would be sacrilege. No one other than the family had any religious role in that property, and, therefore, only the family had any role whatsoever in the property. In other words, much of our Western sense of private property is rooted in the concept of religion and the unique role of the family as a mediating unit in religion.

Among the Romans, this was even more intense. To them, the strong connection among property, family, and religion was evidenced by their view of the family unit: the husband and wife were a priesthood; and while the husband exercised most of the duties of the priesthood, it was a joint priesthood. That is why monogamy was so important to them, for anything else would be a violation of the religious traditions and an interference both with the parents' religious role and its connection to the protection of the family's property.

A Roman who was part of the priesthood — who exercised priestly functions — could not do so after he became widowed; he could only do so as a married man because the loss of his spouse diminished the wholeness of this religious function. Quite often he was succeeded by a married son, who could perform the services. These ideas were very strong at the time of Christ, the Apostles, and the Fathers of the Church, and are a kind of unrecognized sub-stratum to the growth of Christianity. There were aspects of this already in Hebrew thought, forming a natural background for the growth of Christianity.

In the centuries that preceded the birth of Christ, the so-called post-exilic period of the Hebrews, the Jews were permitted under the Persian Empire to return to Judea and proceeded from then on to create a new society. This society was very different from that described, for example, in the Book of Kings and the period of David and Solomon. In this period, there was the growth of conflict between the Sadducees (the priestly class who, for the most part, lived in Jerusalem), on the one hand, and the Pharisees and the pious people in the countryside, on the other, ultimately developing into two religious traditions. A lot of this differentiation was due to the role of the priestly class which combined a sacred function with that of being tax collectors, first for the Persian Empire and later for the successors of Alexander the Great. As tax collectors, they were mixing a sacred and an oppressive function; and if one reads some of the comments of the more pious Jews when they are attacking the rich, they are really attacking those people who were holding official religious offices and yet also oppressing the other part of the population as tax collectors.

These differences also led to differences in religious views, with the Pharisees developing a belief in immortality of the soul and bodily resurrection, and a strong sense of the role of oral tradition in addition to the written Bible in religious affairs. When we come to the birth of Jesus and His emergence in public life, He is articulating in great measure the language of the Pharisees. They are the pious Jews, even though in many areas, as the New Testament shows, they have shifted from what they originally were to being very legalistic and narrow, and therefore are condemned by Jesus in His public ministry.

By the first century, of course, there was a whole new group of tax collectors and publicans, a new rivh. Jesus — if one looks beneath the surface of what was happening — was supported in great measure by His friends and His disciples. We see Jesus and a large group of people who were conducting a very extensive public ministry. They obviously had to live to do that, and the New Testament refers to the people who assisted Jesus, in many cases wealthy women. These people are not condemned for being wealthy because their wealth was being used in a God-ordained manner, *viz.*, to contribute personally to the support of Jesus and His disciples.

And yet, even at that time, not everyone could or was called to do that; people were not condemned for failing to use their wealth to support Jesus and His disciples. This was a special calling. Some accepted it; many others did not. If one examines the New Testament, one finds that there is no condemnation of wealth per se, and there is no attempt to make that a special issue of debate. Christ accepted wealth and He accepted poverty, as He also accepted many things that were neither essentially good nor essentially bad.

When we look at the Epistles of Paul, we find a continuity with Stoic ideas, some of which are very similar to Christian ideas. In particular, Paul refers to the Stoic idea of the importance of self-sufficiency—the importance of people having the property to be self-sufficient and working to achieve enough property to support their family. If people do not do that, they are lacking in the necessary Christian grace. If, on the other hand, they make too much of trying to gain wealth, they are also lacking. But there is no condemnation of wealth as such, and there is a strong emphasis on gaining this kind of self-sufficiency—the basic amount of property needed in order to live consistent with one's society.

Many of the writings of liberation theologians focus mainly on the texts of the Church Fathers, particularly in the fourth century, and if one looks at those texts and does not relate them to what was happening in Roman society during the preceding centuries, one is not going to properly understand them. St. John Chrysostum, St. Basil, or most other of the eastern Fathers, for example, came from monastic backgrounds and a life in which they renounced wealth and took a vow of poverty as a special grace from God. Afterwards they emerged as bishops and spokesmen for the Church. Quite often their language was drawn from that of the concept of monastic poverty.

If one looks deeper into the origins of some of the monastic communities, the earliest monastic communities in the province of Egypt, for example, one finds in the records of the third and fourth centuries that they are first described as similar to the large body of people who fled from their farms into the swamps of the Egyptian delta to escape the tax collectors. Roman society in the second and third centuries had become a society essentially trying to collect taxes. It also became a militarized society in which the soldiers had to be paid large sums, and in order to do that, the whole population was subjected to intense taxation. This reached the level where, in order to collect the taxes, the government assigned leading people—wealthy people in society—great amounts of tax revenue that they were responsible to collect each year. If they did not, it had to come out of their own wealth. And if they did not have sufficient, what wealth they had was confiscated, and they could be sold into slavery. So a system of immense tax collection developed, and with it immense attempts to avoid its cruelty.

When the Fathers of the Church are criticizing the rich for exactions, what they are talking about is the rich who were forced to become tax collectors and, in order to survive, had to make sure everyone else paid taxes. And so there existed a system where all of society was built around the collection and the avoidance of taxes. To avoid the tax collectors, large numbers of people fled from their farms and from the cities, and lived out in the countryside and in the wilderness. Many of these were very religious people, and some of the early monastic communities evolved from these refugees from taxation.

The following are passages from some of the Church Fathers of that period. The first is from the work of Salvian, a fifth-century writer and Church Father, whose book, *The Governance of God*, contains extensive paragraphs on this whole question. He asks, "What is a political position but a kind of plunder? There is no greater pillage of poor states than that done by those in power." He continues, because he is talking about tax collectors, by speaking of those strangled by the chains of taxation as if by the hands of brigands. "There is found a great number of rich whose taxes kill the poor." He then proceeds to say,

What towns, as well as municipalities and villages, are there in which there are not as many tyrants as tax collectors? Perhaps they glory in the name of tyrant because it seems to be considered powerful and honored. What place is there, as I have said, where the bowels of widows and orphans are not devoured by the leading men of the city, and with them of almost all Holy Men? All the while the poor are despoiled, the widows groan, the orphans are tread underfoot, so much that many of them — and they are not of obscure birth and have received a liberal education — flee to the barbarians lest they die from the pain of public persecution. They seek among the barbarians the dignity of the Roman because they cannot bear barbarous indignity among the Romans.

This is the period where the great German tribes were moving into the Roman Empire. One of the surprising aspects of this is that they were welcomed as liberators by most of the Roman citizens because they did not impose the tax structures, the strangling of trade and commerce and wealth, that were imposed by the Roman administration.

Thus, far and wide, they migrate either to the Goths or to the Baghudi, or to other barbarians everywhere in power, yet they do not repent having migrated. They prefer to live as free men under an outward form of captivity, than as captives under an appearance of liberty. Therefore, the name of Roman citizens, not only greatly valued but dearly bought, is now repudiated and fled from—and it is considered not only base but even deserving of abhorrence. And what cannot be a greater testimony of Roman wickedness than that many men, upright and noble and to whom the position of being a Roman citizen should be considered as of the highest splendor and dignity, have been driven by the cruelty of Roman wickedness to such a state of mind that they do not wish to be Romans. Hence, even those who do not flee to the barbarians are forced to be barbarians. Such is the great portion of the Spaniards, not the least portion of the Gauls, and finally all those throughout the whole Roman world whom Roman wickedness has compelled not to be Romans.

In like manner, therefore, the same thing is happening to almost all the lower classes, for they are driven by one cause to two very different choices. The highest force demands that they wish to aspire to liberty, but the same force does not permit them to be able to do what it compels them to wish to do. Perhaps it can be charged against them that they wish to be men who desire nothing more than to be forced to wish for liberty. Their greatest misfortune is what they wish for, for it would be much better for them if they were not compelled to wish for it. But what else can these wretched people wish for? They, who suffer the insistent, and even continuous destruction of public tax levies, to them there is always imminent a heavy and relentless proscription.

They desert their homes, lest they be tortured in their very homes. They seek exile lest they suffer torture. The enemy is more lenient to them than the tax collectors. This is proved by this very fact that they flee to the enemy in order to avoid the full force of the heavy tax levy.

Salvian continues, page after page, describing this condition. Later, when the barbarians settled in the Roman Empire, welcomed by all these people trying to escape the burden of endless torture inflicted to find out if they had hidden wealth, they, as Orosius, a Father of the Church of that period, pointed out, turned to the plow and cherished the Romans as comrades and friends. There could then be found among them certain Romans who preferred poverty with freedom among the barbarians to paying tribute with anxiety among the Romans.

Similar ideas are found in some of the other Church Fathers. When we turn to the writings of Lactantius in the same period, we find a further analysis of this question. He shows that those who advocate community of goods draw this from Plato and from the idea among the Greeks of a Golden Age in which community property existed. He points out that the idea of community property is something that cannot be accepted by Christians. Lactantius also shows that community property is completely connected and integrated with a non-Christian concept of marriage and family, and that Plato, in calling for community of property, also called for community of wives. He explains that that is unnatural, that destruction of private property leads to the destruction of the family, and that if you want to protect the family, you must protect private property. As a Christian Father, he calls out to the Christian world that it must first protect private property if it wants to protect the family from all the assaults that it is suffering in that period.

Lactantius goes on at length to explain the interconnection between ownership and the virtues that come from it, the sound families it produces, and how the assault on it is an assault on Christian virtue. He says, for example, "He who wishes to make men equal, then, ought to withdraw not matrimony, not wealth, but arrogance, pride, boastfulness, so that those powerful and elated men may know that they are equals even of the most beggarly," He also states that the important thing is attitude of mind, i.e., virtue, not the question of equality of property or the creation of common goods. He states, ". . . for ownership of things contains the matter of virtues and of vices, but community holds nothing other than the license of vices." He also points out that private property is a distinguishing quality of men, as opposed to animals, and that this is something of great importance to understand.

Another Church Father to whom I would like to refer is St. Augustine. One of his close friends, Hilarius, who was from Syracuse, wrote a letter to him and said that some Christians Syracuse were saying, "That a rich man who continues to live richly cannot enter the Kingdom of Heaven unless he sells all he has, and that it cannot do him any good to keep the Commandments while keeping his riches."

Augustine answered him at great length in order to supply him with arguments to rebut this. He begins,

> Listen, now, to something about riches in answer to the inquiry in your letter. In it you wrote that some are saying that a rich man who continues to live richly cannot enter the Kingdom of Heaven unless he sells all he has, and that it cannot do him any good to keep the Commandments while he keeps his riches. Their arguments have overlooked our Fathers, Abraham, Isaac, and Jacob, who departed long ago from this life. It is a fact that all these had extensive riches, as the Scripture faithfully bears witness, yet He who became poor for our sake, although he was truly rich, foretold in a manner in a truthful promise that many would come from the East and West and would sit down, not above them, not without them, but with them in the Kingdom of Heaven. Although the haughty rich man who is clothed in purple and fine linen, and feasted sumptuously every day, died and was tormented in Hell, nevertheless, if he had shown mercy to the poor man covered with sores who lay at his door, and was treated with scorn, he himself would have deserved mercy. And if the poor man's merit had been his poverty, not his goodness,

he would surely not have been carried by Angels into the Bosom of Abraham, who had been rich in this life.

This is intended to show us that, on the one hand, it was not poverty in itself that was divinely honored, nor on the other hand, riches that were condemned, but that the godliness of the one and ungodliness of the other had their own consequences. And as the torment of fire was the lot of the ungodly rich man, so the bosom of the rich Abraham received the godly poor man. Although Abraham lived as a rich man, he held his riches so lightly and thought them of so little worth in comparison with the Commandments of God, that he would not offend God by refusing to sacrifice at his bidding the very individual whom he had hoped and prayed for as the heir of his riches.

At this point, Augustine supposes they probably say that the patriarchs of old did not sell all they had to give it to the poor because the Lord had not commanded it. Augustine continues,

But in the New Testament, there is no such requirement. We believe that the Apostle Paul was the minister of the New Testament when he wrote to Timothy, saying, "Charge the rich of this world not to be high-minded, nor to trust in the uncertainty of riches, but in the Living God, who giveth us abundantly all things to enjoy, to do good, to be rich in good works, to give easily to communicate to others, to lay up on store for themselves a good foundation against the time to come, that they may hold on the true life," as it was said to the young man, "if thou will enter into life . . . etc." I think when he gave those instructions to the rich, the apostle was not wrong in not saying, "Charge the rich of this world to sell all they have and give to the poor and follow the Lord," instead of, "not to be high-minded nor to trust in the uncertainty of riches." It was his pride, and not the riches, that brought the rich young man to the torment of Hell because he despised the good poor man who lay at his gate; because he put his hope in the uncertainty of riches and thought himself happy in his purple and fine linen and sumptuous banquet.

Augustine goes on to elaborate further on these points and to show that the question of wealth was not the central issue in the New Testament discussions, but that wealth and poverty were used as figures, as examples, in the presentations.

It is interesting to note that the main sources from which liberation theologians quote are the Greek Fathers of this period who, as I indicated to you, had been brought up in eastern Monasticism. All those from which I have quoted have been western Fathers—Fathers mainly in Gaul, and Augustine in North Africa—who had a very different perspective. It would be worth our examining this phenomenon more closely to find out some of the reasons for this difference between the eastern and the western Church during this period when they are obviously addressing what in some ways were quite similar societies and in other ways very different societies.

The western Fathers and the eastern Fathers were both writing following a period of intense economic disorder caused first of all by taxation, and then, as taxation became an insufficient source of wealth, the continual debasing of the currency by the military emperors. Consequently, there was terrible inflation between 300 B.C., an inflation that was so ravaging that it led to the imposition of price controls by Diocletian. This further disrupted the economy and finally led to those forms of taxation which required that everyone in society either perform compulsory services directly or else contribute money to the state. Everyone was placed into a designated role in the state structure which they could not leave, and from which their children could not deviate. There was, in other words, the beginnings of the feudal society that continued into the Middle Ages.

It was against the background of this extremely violent disruption of society that, as Salvian and Orosius pointed out, many of the Romans wanted to be barbarians because the barbarians were not burdened with all of the government regulations and the debasement of currency. The end result was that the barbarians came into the Roman Empire and settled amidst the Roman population, became Christians, and then this new

Christian society attempted to get out from under the huge debacle created by all of this heavy, immense state taxation.

Now these are issues which are not addressed by the liberation theologians. First, I'd like to call attention to the fact that most of the Roman Catholic liberation theologians come from the religious orders, not the regular diocesan clergy. Even the bishops and cardinals who are defenders of liberation theology have come from religious orders. Some of the Brazilian cardinals, for instance, have been Franciscans. If one looks at the American hierarchy today, one will find a number of Catholic bishops who have been drawn from religious orders. This is a very unique situation; it is not normal and has not happened for hundreds of years. The normal procedure is for the bishops to be drawn from the diocesan clergy; that is, from clergy who have not taken a vow of poverty and who are permitted to own as much or as little as they have, inherit, or earn. They are men who have to deal with the daily problems of the mortgage on the church, the school, the rectory, and the convent.

Previously, the American hierarchy was known throughout the world for being a successful business hierarchy. There was even a certain amount of criticism of the fact that up until recently, American bishops and archbishops were more knowledgeable about real estate, interest rates, and mortgages, than some religious issues. But without that knowledge their churches could not have survived. They would not have been able to minister to their flocks if they could not pay the debt on the mortgage; therefore, since every parish that assumes a mortgage is guaranteed by the diocesan organization—in essence the bishop—the bishop has to know about the financing and maintaining of the properties and buildings of the Churches in his diocese.

The success of the American bishops in building such a strong fiscal and physical foundation, providing churches in which to worship and schools in which to study, was a marvel to the world. This began to change about fifteen years ago. The controversies surrounding the Vietnam War found most of the bishops supporting the policies of the United States government, and this was not viewed either among many of the younger clergy or by Catholic leaders abroad as wise. As a result, the Vatican started looking outside of the diocesan clergy to replace them with people drawn from monasteries.

Archbishop Wheatland, of Milwaukee, for instance, who is the chairman of the commission about to issue the "Pastoral Letter" dealing with economic issues, is from a monastic order. Many of the other new bishops, the younger ones, have been drawn from monastic orders where they have led a life very different from the rest of their flocks. That is unlike the traditional diocesan clergy and bishops, who have normally lived with their parishioners and, in fact, lived a life similar to them in the sense that they were not required to take a vow of poverty. Many of the new bishops, however, are drawn from people who have taken a very special set of vows chosen to set themselves off from the rest of the Catholic population in order to perform more specialized spiritual services and to develop particular spiritual virtues.

But they have now been drawn away from the isolation in which they were supposed to practice those vows, and have been thrown into the midst of the rest of the population. These are people who do not have any close connections with the rest of the Catholic population—either the clergy or the laity. The result is a certain amount of "crisis," which has become more and more intense as their influence has spread more generally among the hierarchy. Some of the new leadership think it was perhaps even sinful for the bishops of previous generations to develop property and to build these churches and schools; that that showed lack of spiritual vision and that they were dealing with Mammon rather than the Spirit. Consequently, there is now a great deal of conflict between the bishops' demands that the laity and the congregations contribute money to vast new programs the former wish to encourage, and the pastors who have to maintain schools and do not like to see their parishioners' money being drained off to the National Conference of Catholic Bishops to be distributed as Third-World alms.

In conclusion, what we have is a vast difference between the first 2,000 years of theology based on individual reform and individual salvation and the current idea of some sort of collective salvation accomplished by changing political and social policies and institutions.

We have among all these people from religious orders a spirit of which the writings in liberation theology are just the tip of the iceberg. Beneath these is a mindset very different from the traditions of the Christian Church and reinforced by all kinds of modern social science dogmas. They have substituted a secular religion of social science for the doctrines of the Christian Church, and they feel that in their hands they have great tools for doing all kinds of marvelous things.

It is important for us to show that the Old Testament and the New Testament and the Fathers of the Church form a tradition concerning wealth and poverty which is consistent with capitalism and inconsistent with modern socialism and communism. We must show that this new theology will bring disaster to the Christian Church whereas the reaffirmation, continuation, and development of traditional theology will lead to the increased spiritual health of both the Church at large and Western society as a whole.

Catholic Social Thought, Virtue and Public Morality

J. Brian Benestad

J. Brian Benestad is associate professor in the department of theology/religious studies at the University of Scranton in Pennsylvania. He received his B.A. from Assumption College, S.T.L. (Licentiate in Theology) from Gregorian University, Rome, Italy (1968), and his Ph.D. in political science from Boston College (1979). Dr. Benestad's fields of specialization are Christianity and political theory; religion and American politics. He has published several papers, articles, and two books on questions of Christianity, politics, and social order from a Catholic perspective. He is an associate of the Center on Religion and Society, and a member of the Pennsylvania Catholic Conference's Department of Justice and Rights.

PART I. THE BISHOPS AND THE COMMON GOOD: EVANGELIZATION, CATHOLIC SOCIAL TEACHING AND POLICY STATEMENTS

In their recent letter on war and peace, the French bishops said:

A people cannot live for a long time with its eyes riveted upon the radar screens of its territorial surveillance or upon the statistical charts of its economists. All this is important but remains in the order of means. Beyond the means of living arises the question of the reasons for living for persons, but also for nations

141

and for the entire human race. And this is a question of culture—that is to say a spiritual question.[1]

The Catholic Church is one of the many institutions in the United States that attempts to provide guidance on spiritual matters, and thus on the great moral questions facing humanity. The first task of Catholic bishops is to preach the Gospel. Therefore, they must be "guides of consciences," to quote Pope John Paul II's recent remarks to the Canadian bishops. Bishops are first and foremost educators in the faith and not politicians. Nevertheless, "evangelization seeks to get to the very core of culture, the realm of basic values, and to bring about a conversion that will serve as a basis and guarantee of a transformation of structures and the social milieu."[2]

As educators in the faith, the bishops must proclaim not only the creed but also the moral teaching of the Church. If the Church educates the faithful well through its bishops, priests and lay collaborators, the whole society will benefit in many ways. The Church's educational task is never finished and admittedly is not done well enough. Even non-Catholics notice that Catholics are not as knowledgeable about their faith as they might be. There are, moreover, Catholic theologians challenging the magisterium of the Church.

In addition to evangelizing its own faithful, the Catholic Church also attempts to address the wider society on matters pertaining to the general welfare or the common good. Hence, the recent pastoral letter on war and peace and the upcoming letter on the economy. Such statements form part of what is known as Catholic social doctrine, which is based not only on revelation but also on reason. Some of the specifically religious teachings are shared with other faiths; teachings based on rea-

---

[1]*Out of Justice, Peace, Joint Pastoral Letter of the West German Bishops Winning the Peace, Joint Pastoral Letter of the French Bishops* (San Francisco: Ignatius Press, 1984) No. 55, p. 118.

[2]John Eagleson and Philip Scharper, eds., *Puebla and Beyond: Documentation and Commentary* (Maryknoll, New York: Orbis Books, 1979), No. 388, p. 177.

son can potentially be shared by all. For many centuries, the Catholic Church has taught, especially through Augustine and Thomas Aquinas, that the pursuit of a just social order requires attention to all aspects of the common good. A focus on the common good in Catholic social teaching leads to discussion of such topics as the following:

- Virtue;
- The duty to make good use of material things and the right to property;
- Life and liberty, including abortion, infanticide, euthanasia, and suicide;
- The social nature of the human person, solidarity and the relation between duties and rights;
- The principle of subsidiarity, including the role of the state;
- The relation of law and morality;
- The family;
- Primary, secondary and higher education;
- Work;
- The differing roles of the laity and the clergy in the temporal order;
- Social justice, legal justice, distributive justice, commutative justice;
- Public morality or public philosophy;
- Fraternity among citizens, and the importance of shared values.

In addition to evangelizing and communicating Catholic social doctrine, the U.S. Catholic bishops have also chosen to promote justice by engaging in partisan politics through the taking of positions on public policy questions. (This kind of activity is normally the role of the laity.) The bishops frequently refer to these positions as prudential judgments. The pastoral letter on war makes a clear reference to the nonbinding character of these prudential judgments.

Since the Second Vatican Council ended, the bishops have unfortunately put too much stress on policy issues. The first draft of the bishops' pastoral on the U.S. economy is not atypical. Even Joseph Califano, former assistant to Lyndon Johnson and former Secretary of HEW, says the following about that draft:

> When the bishops move to what they call policy applications, they sound more like one of the great society legislative messages I helped draft for Lyndon Johnson than a group of clerics calling attention to the moral, religious, and ethical dimensions of the society they are trying to reshape.[3]

Califano goes on to say that the bishops subvert their powerful and desperately needed basic message "by attempting to write legislative and administrative regulations."

In relating faith to public life, the bishops should focus on communicating and developing Catholic social doctrine in all its richness. Catholic social doctrine can even provide a public philosophy for the nation, not only by furnishing guidelines for legislation, but also by shaping the nation's customs. Presenting Catholic social doctrine as a public philosophy may be the most valuable contribution the Church can make to political life in the United States.

It is true that, in stating their own policy positions, the bishops often provide a summary statement of Catholic social principles. Still, the stress on policy leads to the neglect of essential themes in Catholic doctrine. For example, the first draft of the pastoral letter on the U.S. economy contains very little on education, the family or virtue.

Education

Too many students, especially the poor, graduate from grade school and high school without sufficient literacy or culture. Even privileged youth attending college often graduate with little knowledge of the humanities, including literature, philosophy, history and religion.

---

[3]"The Prophets and the Profiters," *America* 152, No. 1 (1985), p. 6.

What does the study of the humanities have to do with the poor and other citizens? If educated young people are to address the problems of society in a serious way, they must begin by inquiring into the meaning of good and evil, noble and bad, just and unjust. It is important to graduate students who not only have an interest in justice, but knowledge as well. Higher education in the humanities is a very important part of the work for justice. In William Bennett's much-discussed report on the humanities, we find the following description.

I would describe the humanities as the best that has been said, thought, written and otherwise expressed about the human experience. The humanities have grappled with life's enduring fundamental questions. What is justice? What should be learned? What deserves to be defended? What is courage? What is love? Why do civilizations flourish? Why do they decline?[4]

Virtue

The draft of the economic pastoral does recognize that the practice of virtue is important for political and social life. In part one, the bishops say that "we can find true identity only 'through a sincere gift' of ourselves."[5] While saying little of the effect of sin on politics and society, they do make the following important observation: "Sin alienates human beings from God and shatters the solidarity of the human community."[6] Nevertheless, conversion and virtue are not major themes of the pastoral nor are they considered very reliable or effective tools in the quest for justice.

Permit me to illustrate these points by referring to several passages of the pastoral. In paragraph 85 in the section on

---

[4]*The Chronicle of Higher Education* 29, No. 14 (1984), p. 17.

[5]U.S. Catholic Bishops, *Pastoral Letter on Catholic Social Teaching and the U. S. Catholic Social Teaching and the U. S. Economy, First Draft Origins,* 14, No. 22/23 (1984), par. 24, p. 343, citing Vatican Council II, *Pastoral Constitution on the Church in the Modern World*, 24.

[6]*Ibid.* par. 34, p. 345.

principles, the bishops say that "there are forms of individual and group selfishness present in the nation that undermine social solidarity and efforts to protect the economic rights of all." To overcome individual and group selfishness, the bishops suggest the formation of a new cultural consensus which states:

> All persons really do have rights in the economic sphere and that society has a moral obligation to take the necessary steps to insure that no one among us is hungry, homeless, unemployed, or otherwise denied what is necessary to live with dignity.[7]

This could conceivably be a good political suggestion, but should it be the first reaction of Catholic bishops to selfishness? Even Socrates said that it is worse to do an injustice than to suffer one. Closer to home, Augustine said more than once that "every sin is more hurtful to the sinner than to the sinned against." Should not the Church first try to overcome selfishness by preaching conversion and showing the way to virtue?

The bishops even treat the formation of a cultural consensus as though it were a technical problem similar to revising tax codes. They write:

> Both our cultural values and our tax structures need to be revised to discourage excessively high levels of consumption and to encourage saving and consequent investment in both private and public endeavors that promote the economic rights of all persons.[8]

Cultural values or the nation's customs are surely not formed and ameliorated in the way tax codes are. Later in the same section on principles, the bishops recommend voluntary action in the form of almsgiving, sharing possessions, and hospitality as means of providing some relief to victims of injustice. Acts of charity, however, do not, in their opinion, get at the causes of injustice. They can be removed only "through government and

---

[7]*Ibid.* par. 86, p. 350.
[8]*Ibid.* par. 142, p. 357.

the political process."[9] The bishops imply that securing the proper laws and structures through wise public policy is the only way to get at the root of society's problems. Given such a perspective, it is understandable why the section on principles continually strays into the policy area and why fully half the letter is devoted to policy proposals.

The long Catholic tradition does not support the view that a cultural consensus is revised like a tax code nor that removing the root causes of injustice depends primarily on framing the right laws. On this point, Cardinal Ratzinger distills the best of Catholic political wisdom in the following statement from his "Instruction on Certain Aspects of the Theology of Liberation."

> Nor can one localize evil principally or uniquely in bad social, political or economic "structures" as though all other evils come from them so that the creation of the "new man" would depend on the establishment of different economic and socio-political structures. To be sure, there are structures which are evil and which cause evil and which we must have the courage to change. Structures, whether they are good or bad, are the result of man's actions and so are consequences more than causes. The root of evil, then, lies in free and responsible persons who have to be converted by the grace of Jesus Christ in order to live and act as new creatures in the love of neighbor and in the effective search for justice, self-control and the exercise of virtue.[10]

In his recent "Apostolic Exhortation on Reconciliation and Penance," John Paul II endorses Ratzinger's views on the relation between personal and social evil, and then adds the following:

> At the heart of every situation of sin are always to be found sinful people. So true is this that even when such a situation can be changed in its structure and institutional aspects by the force of law or—as unfortunately more often happens—by the law of force, the change in fact proves to be incomplete, of short dura-

---

[9]*Ibid.* par. 124, p. 355.
[10]*Origins* 14, No. 13 (1984), 197.

tion and ultimately vain and ineffective — not to say
counterproductive — if the people directly or indirectly responsible for that situation are not converted.[11]

The long-standing Catholic tradition mentioned by the bishops reminds us of truths that are still pertinent, though discovered and discussed in other historical eras. Common sense even
used to dictate that vices have social, economic and political
consequences. Everyone can think of examples to show the
baneful influence of pride or excessive ambition, greed, laziness, envy, and anger, not to mention lust and intemperance.
Surely, much work is done incompetently, or not at all, because
of laziness or greed. Does not incompetent work have a devastating effect on the economy and on people's personal lives? Do
not perverted passions lead to child abuse, child pornography
and rape?

Just as sin alienates human beings from God and from one
another, virtue fosters communion and unity. Traditional Catholic teaching on virtue is an implicit criticism of Kantian autonomy, a concept that dominates moral thinking today. In fact,
the great shadow of Immanuel Kant looms so large over moral
and political philosophy that the current stress in Catholic circles on human rights, along with the relative neglect of virtue,
might ultimately serve Kantian, rather than Christian, ends.

PART II. CITIZENS, POLITICIANS AND
THE COMMON GOOD

Introduction

The obligation of all Catholics to promote the common good
is perhaps the benchmark of perennial Catholic wisdom. Com-
menting on the parable of the talents, Chapter 25 of the gospel
of Matthew, John Chrysostom writes: "For nothing is so pleas-

---

[11]*Origins* 14, No. 27 (1984), 442.

ing to God, as to live for the common advantage."[12] Chrysostom explains that all Christians are expected to put their resources and talents at the service of the common good. Recent Catholic social thought has spoken of this obligation under the rubric of social justice. Pius XI said of this virtue, "It is of the very essence of social justice to demand from each individual all that is necessary for the common good." Social justice, rightly understood, directs the acts of all the virtues to the common good. Not everyone has the same obligations, but all are bound to do what is possible. There are many small and great things that can be done by individuals, alone, in various associations, and even through law. To produce social justice, individuals must take initiatives, sometimes heroic. They need not wait, and cannot wait, for specific instructions from bishops and priests. Catholics do, however, need general instruction in Catholic social teaching from their bishops and priests. Knowledge of that teaching will help Catholics, and non-Catholics, to identify the various aspects of the common good. Adapting Catholic wisdom on the exigencies of the common good to the needs and possibilities of a liberal democracy, marked by some disagreement on fundamental matters, is a task for the virtue of prudence. One important way Catholic citizens and politicians can promote the common good is by fostering consensus on shared values, both on evils to be avoided and goods to be sought.

Catholics and other citizens have been trying to promote the common good by opposing the legalization of abortion. In the few remaining pages of my paper, I will explain some of the arguments advanced to show that abortion cannot simply be a private choice.

---

[12]*Homilies on the Gospel of Saint Matthew* (Grand Rapids: William B. Eerdman's Publishing Company, 1956), p. 472. These homilies were originally delivered in the latter part of the fourth century.

Negative and Positive Precepts

Many ask why the bishops do not advocate specific military or economic policies with the same stress and authority that they condemn abortion. No one is in favor of nuclear war or poverty. But political candidates and citizens do legitimately disagree about the best way to promote peace and prosperity. With respect to abortion, the major argument is not about which law should be passed to stop abortion, but whether the unborn deserve any legal protection at all. If laws were passed protecting war, poverty, racism, rape, etc., the bishops would be heard in the same manner as they are on abortion.

It is interesting that negative precepts can be stated more easily than affirmative duties. Regarding the predominance of negative precepts in the decalogue (eight out of ten), Thomas Aquinas makes this thought-provoking observation:

> Man is bound towards all persons in general to inflict injury on no one: hence the negative precepts, which forbid the doing of those injuries that can be inflicted on one's neighbor, had to be given a place as general precepts among the precepts of the decalogue. On the other hand, the duties we owe to our neighbor are paid in different ways to different people: hence it did not behoove to include affirmative precepts about these duties among precepts of the decalogue.[13]

If a negative precept is heeded, the evil stops. If people shun abortion as an evil, or if abortion is prohibited by law, the evil stops.

Law and Morality

The Catholic Church does oppose abortion on religious grounds, as do people of other faiths. However, the Church also teaches that the widespread practice of abortion is a matter

---

[13]II, II, Q. 122, Art. 6. Reply Obj. 1.

of public concern and, therefore, cannot be removed from public debate by labeling it a private choice. By arguing that abortion is a question of public morality, and not simply a religious issue, the bishops are taking abortion out of the category of personal political preference. They are saying that abortion is not an issue on which people should necessarily and legitimately disagree.

Abortion destroys an unborn child, a human being with potential, not a potential human being. Abortion should be no more a matter of personal choice than torture, racism, the intentional killing of the innocent in war or terroristic actions, perjury, theft, rape, etc. Last August, Bishop Malone, speaking for the National Conference of Catholic Bishops, said that he and his fellow bishops reject "the idea that candidates satisfy the requirements of rational analysis in saying their personal views should not influence their policy decisions."[14] The absurdity of that position is suggested by imagining a candidate who makes the following statement: "I am personally opposed to child abuse but will not impose my personal morality on others." Furthermore, it is illogical for political candidates to say that abortion is not a fit subject for public policy because opposition to abortion is based on religious convictions, and then take pride in their own religiously grounded support for social programs to help the needy or for policies to lessen the danger of nuclear war. Those supporting a right to abortion should explain why abortion is not wrong, or why personal choice should outweigh the evil of abortion, or why abortion is one of those evils that the government should not attempt to prevent.

Some do argue that no one can ever know for sure whether the fetus is a person from the moment of conception. Neither philosophy, nor theology, nor science, so the argument runs, can ever definitively resolve the question. "From a moral point of view this is certain: even if a doubt existed concerning whether the fruit of conception is already a person, it is objec-

---

[14]Bishop James Malone, "Religion and the '84 Campaign," *Origins* 14, No. 11 (1984), 163.

tively a grave sin to dare to risk murder."[15] Even the civil law does not allow a person to act in a reckless manner and, thereby, endanger someone's life. You cannot shoot a bullet through a closed door, wound or kill someone and then claim immunity from prosecution because of ignorance.

I am aware that not every evil should be proscribed by law. As Thomas Aquinas said:

> Human law is framed for a number of human beings, the majority of whom are not perfect in virtue. Wherefore human laws do not forbid all vices from which the virtuous abstain, but only the more grievous vices from which it is possible for the majority to abstain; and chiefly those that are to the hurt of others, without the prohibition of which human society could not be maintained: thus human law prohibits murder, theft, and suchlike.[16]

Since abortion does hurt another human being, the child in the womb, it is a fit subject for legislation.

A recent op-ed piece in *The New York Times* made almost the same point about the relation between law and morality as Aquinas did.

> The proper dichotomy is not, as some contend, between law and morality: most laws are grounded in moral concepts. Instead it is between moral principles that relate to the individual conduct of one's own life, with which the law should not deal, and moral principles that relate to actions that may cause harm to others, with which the law must deal.[17]

Aquinas also adds, citing Isadore, that "law should be possible according to nature, and according to the customs of the country." Do the present mores of the nation make legislation

---

[15]Austin Flannery, O. P., ed., "Declaration On Procured Abortion" (Nov. 18, 1984), in *Vatican Council II More Post Counciliar Documents*, Vol. 2, (Northport, New York: 1982), p. 446.

[16]I, II, Q. 96, Art. 2.

[17]Burke J. Balch, "Abortion: A General Concern," *The New York Times*, Vol. 134, Sept. 20, 1984, p. A31.

against abortion unwise or unfeasible? I do not think so. If the Supreme Court decision, *Roe* v. *Wade*, which created a constitutional right to abortion on request, were overturned, we could see whether Americans support federal and state legislation restricting legal access to abortion. In the absence of *Roe* v. *Wade*, Americans could give informed consent to the policies on abortion they want.

Abortion and Other Moral Evils

Public debate on abortion has focused predominantly on the rights of the fetus versus the right to privacy of the woman. There are other serious considerations that need more attention. First, Socrates told us that to do an injustice is worse than to suffer one. Abortions not only violate the rights of fetuses, but also injure all those who perform them, have them, or simply stand by and allow them to continue. Human beings are so constituted that, if they kill their offspring, they do even more serious injury to themselves. To illustrate the point, consider the following true incident that took place in a Nazi prison camp, as recounted by Father James Burtchaell.

> A Dutch woman imprisoned in a Nazi concentration camp was standing barefoot in the snow with other inmates in a punishing session one freezing day when she heard her sister murmuring beside her, "Oh, those poor people; those poor, poor people!" It finally dawned on her that her sister's pity and sympathy were reaching out, not to the hundreds of suffering prisoners, but to the immensely more pitiable soldiers who were tormenting them. The prisoners were suffering pain, but their tormentors were suffering personal damage.[18]

If abortion is indeed wrong, and Burtchaell's observations are correct, then we are doing great harm to ourselves as a nation.

Second, some of the reasons advanced to justify abortion are

---

[18]James T. Burtchaell, "Abortion, Why It Can't be Left to 'personal choice,' " *Catholic Update* 104 (October 1984).

the same used now and in the past to justify infanticide, suicide and euthanasia. For example, killing handicapped children by omitting corrective surgery and/or failure to feed has been justified by doctors and ethicists on these grounds: the lives of handicapped children are a burden both on themselves and on others, including parents, siblings and society. People are beginning to say openly that they will seriously consider suicide if life becomes too burdensome, or if they become burdens to others. (There is, of course, an oft-unnoticed irony in this kind of argument. Those who talk of committing suicide out of love for their family and friends are subtly putting pressure on their loved ones to do the same for them.)

If the practice of abortion continues, there will very likely be increasing pressure on society and the law to sanction infanticide and euthanasia. In an article defending the Indiana court decision to allow the so-called Bloomington baby to starve to death, Peter Singer, a prominent ethicist, wrote:

> If we compare a severely defective human infant with a non-human animal, a dog or a pig, for example, we will often find the non-human to have superior capacities, both actual and potential, for rationality, self-consciousness, communication, and anything else that might be considered morally significant. Only the fact that the defective infant is a member of the species Homo Sapiens leads it to be treated differently from the dog or pig. . . . Humans who bestow superior value on the lives of all human beings solely because they are members of our own species, are judging along lines strikingly similar to those used by white racists who bestow superior value on the lives of other whites, merely because they are members of their own race.[19]

Third, to stem the tide of abortion is to take a public stand against a skewed notion of self-determination. Relativism, both in ethical theory and political life, has led to a greatly exaggerated stress on autonomy in personal actions to the detriment

---

[19]Mary Tedeschi, "Infanticide and Its Apologists," *Commentary* 78, No. 5, pp. 33–34.

even of one's family, friends, and society. "Who is to judge whether the fetus is a human being, or whether a certain material is pornographic?" asks the liberal. On this point, Harvard philosopher Michael Sandel has given one appropriate response.

> It is a question that can be asked of the values that liberals defend. Toleration and freedom and fairness are values too, and they can hardly be defended by the claim that no values can be defended. So it is a mistake to affirm liberal values by arguing that all values are merely subjective. The relativist defense of liberalism is no defense at all.[20]

Still another reason to oppose abortion is to reinforce the teaching that we are our brother's keeper and owe each person his or her due. Parenthood requires that mothers and fathers be prepared to put the needs of their children ahead of their own wants.

---

[20]Michael Sandel, "Morality and the Liberal Ideal," *The New Republic* 190, No. 18, p. 15.

Catholics and Evangelicals: A New Era?

James Hitchcock

James Hitchcock is professor of history at St. Louis University. He is chairman of the Board of the Catholic League for Religious and Civil Rights, and has served as president of the Fellowship of Catholic Scholars as well as editor of *Communio*. He received his A.B. from St. Louis University (1960) and his M.A. (1962) and Ph.D. (1965) from Princeton University. His articles have appeared in a wide variety of journals, including *New York Times Magazine*, *Yale Review*, *Commentary*, *National Review*, *American Scholar*, and *Journal of the American Academy of Religion*. He has authored six books, among them *Catholicism and Modernity* (1979), *What is Secular Humanism?* (1983), and *Who is for Peace?* (1983) with Francis Schaeffer and Vladimir Bukovsky.

Religious differences between Roman Catholics and Evangelical Protestants on one level appear so deep that it scarcely seems necessary to catalogue them.

The most obvious are certain Catholic doctrines such as the authority of the Pope, the sacramental priesthood, and the Mass. However, other, less obvious, differences underlie these.

Differing understandings of the Church itself explain most of the doctrinal differences. Roman Catholicism has tended to celebrate the "visible Church" — organized and incarnate — while the Protestant tradition has tended to see this visible church as a mere historical arrangement, far less important than the "invisible Church" of the saints.

The Catholic sense of tradition underlies certain Catholic beliefs not shared by Evangelicals. This goes beyond mere reverence for the past, which is shared by many people who are not

Catholics. Catholic traditionalism is the principle that the teachings and practices of the Church over time themselves have normative authority in determining what belongs to the authentic Gospel. This in turn must be contrasted with the Protestant principle of *"sola scriptura."*

In practice the Roman Catholic Church places much greater emphasis on the celebration and administration of the sacraments than do most Evangelicals. Catholicism recognizes seven sacraments, adding Confirmation, Holy Orders, Matrimony, and the Last Anointing, in contrast to the general Protestant acceptance of Baptism and the Eucharist. In addition, the Eucharist is the normal daily worship of Catholics, celebrated everywhere where there is a priest, and noneucharistic services are both rarer than the Mass and less important. In practice, Evangelical Protestantism has emphasized the centrality of the preaching of the Word, without ignoring the sacraments, while Roman Catholicism has done the reverse.

Although it does not reach to the level of dogma as such, Catholicism and Evangelicalism have often differed in their attitudes toward secular culture. Catholicism over the centuries has usually favored an approach which could be called the baptizing of the profane, while classical Protestantism has insisted that Divine Revelation is a truth which should not be diluted.

The implications of this principle are many. It has led Catholicism, for example, not only to accept but even to embrace religious art, and to lavish tremendous attention on places of worship. Following the conversion of the Emperor Constantine, the Catholic Church systematically adapted many elements of ancient pagan civilization — art, philosophy, law, political organization — to its own uses.

The adaptation of pagan philosophy, particularly that of Plato by St. Augustine and of Aristotle by St. Thomas Aquinas, is perhaps the most momentous example of how Catholic theology, for better or for worse, has developed in large measure through the use of categories of secular philosophy applied to the understanding of Divine Revelation, while to many Protestants this has seemed almost blasphemous.

On the practical level this has led to a heavy Catholic emphasis on what is called "natural law" — the claim that the essential truths of moral right and wrong are knowable by human beings through reason, even apart from Divine Revelation, so that Catholic moralists have expended a great deal of energy expounding purely philosophical arguments for and against particular human practices.

To some Protestants this seems like a worldly enterprise which does indeed dilute the Gospel. Even many Catholics have been critical of what is called "casuistry" (from the Latin word for "case") — a system of moral reasoning which seeks to provide formulas which can be applied in every conceivable moral situation, and to devise rules which can be invoked to resolve difficulties. The Catholic response, while acknowledging the dangers of a wholly secular approach to morality and also the danger of sterile legalism which casuistry contains, has been to say that human beings in the world need practical guidance, and that the general teachings of the Gospel need to be applied in specific situations, using secular insights where these are helpful.

Finally, Protestant–Catholic differences can perhaps be traced to a single profound difference which dramatically manifested itself at the time of the Reformation — differing attitudes to the ma erial world. Roman Catholicism has been preeminently a religion which insists that everything spiritual must be expressed materially — in symbol, in sacrament, in ritual, in visible structure and hierarchy, in law — while classical Protestantism has required an austerely spiritual religion, with faith as an interior disposition of the soul based on direct and unmediated response to the Word of God.

The past quarter century has brought about a significant softening of differences between Catholics and Protestants.

On the Catholic side, the Second Vatican Council (1962–65) took considerable pains to overcome at least those Protestant–Catholic differences which were based on misunderstanding or on un-Christian mistrust. This was true not only on the level of encouraging ecumenical discussion and cooperation but, more importantly, by a renewed emphasis on Scripture, and particularly by the affirmation that Scripture and tradition are not to be considered two parallel sources of authority, as they were often understood to be in the past. Tradition was affirmed to be nothing more than the Church's own understanding of, and reflection upon, the Scriptures. There is no doubt that, since the early 1960s, many religious barriers have been broken down.

On the Evangelical side there have been signs of a desire to move closer to a Catholic position, in the sense of a greater emphasis on the visible Church, on worship, and on sacraments. The charismatic movement has proven to be an important meeting ground for Catholics and Evangelicals.

Prior to the 1960s the major movement within Christianity seemed to be toward the liturgical, dogmatic, tradition-minded churches—Roman Catholic, Eastern Orthodox, Anglican. Beginning in the mid-nineteenth century there was a whole series of distinguished intellectual converts who embraced "high church" Christianity not in spite of its rituals and dogma but in a sense almost because of them. For whatever reason, this was the mode of Christian belief and life which for a long time seemed most attractive and most credible.

Since about 1960, however, much of the "action" within Christianity has taken place in the evangelical mode, which stresses personal religious experience, direct and individual approach to God, and the centrality of the Scriptures. The "externals" of religion have, in this mode, usually been deemed unimportant.

It is not easy to account for shifts in religious sensibility of this kind, but there is no doubt that such a shift has occurred, to the point, for example, where much of the vitality in contemporary Catholicism derives from the charismatic movement.

There has also been a coming together of Catholics and Evangelicals motivated by what might be called negative factors, namely, a growing recognition of the threats to Christianity itself posed both by the secular culture and by liberal Christianity.

Liberal Christianity can be defined as the assumption that

religion is under an obligation to adapt itself completely to changing cultures. Ultimately, it does not believe in transcendent divine revelation but conceives religion as born out of the ongoing "religious consciousness" of the human race. Virtually everything in religion, including finally even God, is regarded as a human creation, which human beings therefore can, and even must, change in order to meet changing human needs. By contrast, orthodox Christians believe that the source of their religion is God's self-revelation of Himself to His people.

It is at this point — whether or not God truly reveals Himself, or whether what is called revelation is merely a human discovery not essentially different from the most profound philosophy and poetry — that the widest gulf exists in contemporary Christianity. It is not a gulf which runs between denominations, but cuts across practically all denominations, running through the middle of many. When this is understood, it is obvious why many Catholics now feel that they have more in common with many Evangelicals than with some members of their own church, and vice versa.

This common core of faith does not need to be rehearsed, since it is that which is contained in the historic creeds. At a minimum that core includes belief in the Trinity, in the historical Incarnation, in Jesus Christ as both God and man and as savior, in Original Sin, in the divine authority of the Scripture, the Virgin Birth, and in Christ's historical resurrection from the dead.

Obviously such a creed still leaves much about which orthodox Catholics and orthodox Evangelicals might disagree, and most of their disagreements are not unimportant (for example, over the office of the papacy, or over the number and meaning of the sacraments). However, it is equally obvious that this common core provides much greater unity even across denominational lines than orthodox Catholics and orthodox Evangelicals are likely to find with liberal members of their own churches who either reject tenets of the creed or interpret them in ways which undermine their traditional meaning.

Modern Evangelicalism has been particularly sensitive to the dangers of "demythologizing" the Scriptures, a practice engaged in by liberal theologians and biblical scholars. It is a process which has belatedly entered Roman Catholicism as well, so that some Catholic biblical scholars appear to be running very hard to catch up with a century of liberal Protestant exegesis.

Orthodox Roman Catholics have also become aware of how the activity of demythologizing is being systematically applied to the Church — to its doctrines, its structure, and its history — in order to discredit ecclesiastical authority in the eyes of ordinary believers. Both Catholics and Evangelicals should be aware of how far the liberal agenda of demythologizing now extends. It aims finally to leave no religious stone standing upon another. Part of the wider modernist agenda is the discrediting of all moral and spiritual absolutes, and liberal Christianity, according to script, plays that role with respect to religion. Thus there is not even a possible basis for compromise between orthodox and liberal Christians, because liberal religion, in order to be true to its own principles, must ultimately call into question everything which has been believed. To a great extent liberal Christians operate within the Christian framework only because it is the one they have inherited and which fits their culture, not because they necessarily concede it any transcendent validity.

Inevitably, the most sensitive point in all this is practical morality, especially that area of morality which is always the most sensitive and emotional, because the most personal — sex. It is at this point that the modern secular world, often abetted by liberal Christians, has chosen to assault the Christian view of life most sharply and directly, and where it has arguably done the most damage. (When people change their patterns of sexual behavior, they tend to change their beliefs also.)

Except for contraception, orthodox Catholics and orthodox Evangelicals broadly agree on the basic principles, and most of the applications, of sexual morality, and can join in a common struggle both to defend the ideal of Christian chastity from the various attacks made on it and to make that ideal plausible and appealing to the contemporary world. Abortion has been the most sensitive and the most urgent of those issues, an issue where there is already substantial Catholic and Evangelical cooperation. This area of common struggle is likely to get broader rather than narrower in the years ahead, as infanticide and euthanasia gain increasing respectability in Western society.

Modern ecumenism dates from certain attempts at cooperation across denominational lines first made prior to World War I. The period since the Second Vatican Council has often been called the Age of Ecumenism, and so highly publicized has been this activity that many people assume that all of the important work has already been done, so that ecumenical activity now has a slightly outdated and anticlimactic character to it.

Arguably, however, the real Age of Ecumenism is just beginning, in that the real ecumenical frontier lies not between liberal Protestantism and liberal Catholicism, whose adherents have often reached agreement by proclaiming the equal irrelevance of both their religious traditions, but between orthodox Catholics and orthodox Evangelicals, who take their faith seriously.

As true ecumenism is bound to be, this is a phenomenon containing both pleasant surprises and frustrating problems. On the one hand Catholics and Evangelicals do understand one another better, and have found more basis for common agreement and common action than anyone thought possible a quarter of a century ago. On the other hand, precisely because both sides in this encounter do take their faith very seriously, and do not believe that they are permitted to compromise that faith for the sake of agreement, this ecumenical discussion will take many years.

It is likely to be the only kind of ecumenical discussion which will mean anything, however, by the end of this century, since it is a dialogue between two groups of people who still willingly and meaningfully claim for themselves the title of Christians. For the logic of liberal Christianity, on both the Catholic and Protestant sides, now leads merely to a progressive watering down of Christian beliefs to conform to the changing spirit of the times and even to a final acquiescence in the emergence of a post-Christian age.

Index

165